Foster Barham Zincke

A Month in Switzerland

Foster Barham Zincke

A Month in Switzerland

ISBN/EAN: 9783337152109

Printed in Europe, USA, Canada, Australia, Japan

Cover: Foto ©Andreas Hilbeck / pixelio.de

More available books at **www.hansebooks.com**

A MONTH IN SWITZERLAND

BY

F. BARHAM ZINCKE
VICAR OF WHERSTEAD
CHAPLAIN IN ORDINARY TO THE QUEEN

Deo Opt. Max.

LONDON
SMITH, ELDER, & CO., 15 WATERLOO PLACE
1873

All rights reserved

PREFACE

THE LEGITIMATE USE of a Preface, like that of a Prologue, is merely to give explanations that will be necessary, and to save from expectations that would be delusive. I will, therefore, at once say to those who may have read my 'Egypt of the Pharaohs and of the Kedivé,' that this little book belongs to the same family. The cast of thought and the aims of the two are kindred, and both endeavour to do their work by similar methods. They are, alike, efforts to attain to a right reading, and a right interpretation of nature, and of man. The differences between them are, perhaps, such as must result from the differences in the matter itself they had, respectively, to take account of. The field, in which the younger sister here makes some studies, is small in extent;

its physical conditions, too, are those of our own part of the world, and its human issues those of our own times. It ought, therefore, to be looked at from very near points of view, and to be exhibited in pictures of much detail and minuteness. The field, however, which the elder sister surveyed, was wide in area, and rich with scenes of singularly varied character. Its place, indeed, in the panorama of nature possesses an interest which is exclusively its own ; and its history includes a chapter in the construction of thought and of society, of which—while again its own with almost equal exclusiveness—the right appreciation is necessary for the right understanding of some contemporary and subsequent chapters in general history, and not least of the one that is at this day unfolding itself, with ourselves for the actors, we being, also, at the same time, the material dealt with, and fashioned. So it presented itself to my own mind, and so I attempted to set it before the reader's mind.

To those, however, who are unacquainted with the book I have just referred to in explanation of the character and aims of its successor, I would describe the impulse under which both of them were written in the familiar words, 'My heart was hot within me ; and, while I was thus musing, the fire kindled, and at the last I spake with my tongue.' I had been much stirred by a month spent among the Swiss mountains, not only by what might have been their effect upon me had I been alone, but also by what I had seen of their effect upon others—to one of whom, a child who was with me throughout the excursion (if mention of so small a matter, as it may appear to some, can be allowed), a little space has been given in the following pages ; and this it was that first made me wish to fix in words the scenes I had passed through, the impressions I had received from them, and the thoughts that had grown out of them. But how unlike was the landscape, and those who peopled it, to what had come before the eye, and the mind's eye, in Egypt ! Instead of the long life-giving river and the broad life-repelling desert, both so replete with history, the import of which is not yet dead, as well as with natural phenomena of an unwonted character to eyes familiarised with the aspects of our little sea-girt sanctuary, as we fondly deem it, Switzerland offered for contemplation, in the order of nature, the ice and snow world of its cloud-piercing mountains ; and, in the order of what is of existing human concern, unflagging industry, patient frugality, intelligently-adapted education, a natural form of land-tenure, and popular government; and invited the spectator of its scenery, as well as of the social and intellectual fermentation of portions of its people, in strong contrast to the immobility of other portions, to meditate on some of the new elements, which modern knowledge, and modern conditions of society, may have contributed for the enlargement and rectification of some of our religious ideas, inclusive, and, perhaps, above all, of our idea of God; for these ideas have at every epoch of man's history been, more or less, modified by contemporary knowledge, and the contemporary conditions of society. These were the materials for thought Switzerland supplied. Upon all of those, however, which belong to the order of human concern, Egypt, too, in its sense and fashion, had had something to tell us.

As to the form and colouring of the work, I could have wished that there had been, throughout, submitted to the reader's attention nothing but the scenes described, and the thoughts they gave rise to, without any suggestion, had that been possible, of the writer's personality. In a work of this kind a vain wish: for in all books, those only excepted that are simply scientific, and in the highest degree in those that deal with matter, in which human interests preponderate, the personality of the writer must be seen in everything he writes. All that he describes is described as he saw and observed it. Others would have observed things differently. So, too, with what he thought about them; it must be different from what others would have thought. A book of this kind must, therefore, be, to a great extent, a fragment of autobiography, in which, for the time, the inner is seen in its immediate relation to the external life of the author. It gives what he felt and thought; his leanings, and likings, and wishes; his readings of the past and of the present; and his mental moorings. This—and especially is it so on a subject with which everyone is familiar, though it may be one that can never be worn out—is all he properly has to say. And his having something of this kind to say, is his only justification for saying anything at all. The expectation, too, of finding that he has treated matters a little in this way is, in no small degree, what induces people to give a hearing to what he says. They take up his book just because they have reason for supposing that he has regarded things from his own point of view, and so seen them from a side, and in a light, and in relations to connected subjects, somewhat different from those in which other people, themselves included, may have seen them; and that he has, therefore, taken into his considerations and estimates some particulars they must have omitted in theirs. Whether his ideas are to the purpose, whether they will hold water, whether they will work, the reader will decide for himself. But in whatever way these questions may be answered, one particular, at all events, is certain, a book of this kind must be worthless, if it is not in some sort autobiographical; while, if it is, it may, possibly, be worth looking over. On no occasion, therefore, have I hesitated to set down just what I thought and felt, being quite sure that this is what every reasonable reader wishes every writer to do.

One more preliminary note. I was accompanied by my wife and stepson, the little boy just now mentioned, who was between nine and ten years of age. Switzerland was not new ground to any one of the three. Occasionally a carriage was used. When that was not done I always walked. My wife was on foot for about half the distance travelled over. The little boy, when a carriage was not used, almost always rode. I give these particulars in order that any family party, that might be disposed to extract from the following pages a route for a single excursion, might understand what they could do, and in what time and way it could be done. The August and September of the excursion were those of last year, 1872.

F. B. Z.

WHERSTEAD VICARAGE:
    January 16, 1873.

CONTENTS.

CHAPTER I.

To Zermatt 1

CHAPTER II.

The Riffel—The Gorner Grat—Sunday—Zermatt—Schwarz See—Mountaineering 11

CHAPTER III.

Walk back to St. Niklaus—Agriculture—Life—Religion in the Valley 21

CHAPTER IV.

I. Peasant-proprietorship in the Valley—II. Landlordism—III. The Era of Capital—IV. Obstructions to the free Interaction of Capital and Land—Their Effects and probable Removal—V. Co-operative Farming not a Step forward 28

CHAPTER V.

Walk to Saas im Grund—Fee, and its Glacier—The Mattmark'See 113

CHAPTER VI.

Walk over Monte Moro to Macugnaga, Ponte Grande, and Domo d'Ossola 122

CHAPTER VII.

Walk over the Simplon 131

CHAPTER VIII.

Brieg—Upper Rhone Valley by Char *to the Rhone Glacier—Hôtel du Glacier du Rhône* 140

CHAPTER IX.

Walk over the Grimsel, by the Aar Valley, Helle Platte, and the Falls of Handeck, to Meiringen . . . 149

CHAPTER X.

Char *to Interlaken—Walk over the Wengern Alp to Grindelwald* 155

CHAPTER XI.

*Interlaken—*Char *up the Valley of the Kander—Walk over the Gemmi, sleeping at Schwarenbach* 163

CONTENTS

CHAPTER XII.
Leukabad—Aigle 172

CHAPTER XIII.
The Drama of the Mountains 184

CHAPTER XIV.
On Swiss Hotels 194

CHAPTER XV.
Berne—Swiss Fountains—Zurich—Museum of Relics from ancient Lake-villages—Baur en ville—*Récolte des Voyageurs—C'est un pauvre Pays* 205

CHAPTER XVI.
A Remark on Swiss Education 218

CHAPTER XVII.
Elsass—Lothringen—Metz—Gravelotte—Mother of the Curé of Ste. Marie aux Chênes—Waterloo . . . 230

CHAPTER XVIII.
How the Observation and Knowledge of Nature, and the Conditions of Society, affect Religion and Theology—An instructive Parallelism—Conclusion 250

INDEX 265

A MONTH IN SWITZERLAND

CHAPTER I.

TO ZERMATT

> What blessings Thy free bounty gives
> Let me not cast away;
> For God is paid when man receives:
> T' enjoy is to obey.—POPE.

August 26.—We left London at 8.45 P.M., and reached Paris the next morning at 7 A.M. We found the Capua of the modern world looking much as it used to look in the days that preceded the siege and the Commune. The shops were decked, and the streets were peopled, much in the old style. If, as we are told, frivolity, somewhat tinctured with, or, at all events, tolerant of, vice, together with want of solidity and dignity of character, are as conspicuous as of yore in the Parisian, we may reply that if they were there before, they must be there still; for a people can no more change on a sudden the complexion of their thoughts and feelings than they can the complexion of their faces. These matters are in the grain, and are traditional and hereditary. The severity of taxation France will have to submit to may, when it shall have made itself felt, have some sobering effect, whereas the bribery and corruption of the Imperial *régime* only acted in the contrary direction. But time is needed for enabling this to become a cause of change; and much may arise, at any moment, in the volcanic soil of France, to disturb its action. All that we can observe at present is, that the people seem still quite unconscious of the causes of their great catastrophe. Their talk, when it refers to late events, is of treason and of revenge; as if they had been betrayed by anything but their own ignorance, arrogance, and corruption; and as if revenge, to be secured, had only to be desired. In such talk, if it indicates what is really thought and felt, there is scant ground for hope.

August 27.—We left Paris this evening at eight o'clock, taking the route of Dijon and Pontarlier. The sun was up when we reached Switzerland at Verrieres. There was no gradation in the scenery: as soon as we were on Swiss ground it became Swiss in character—mountainous and rocky, with irrigated meadows of matchless green in the valley. We were sure that the good people in the *châlets* below could not be otherwise than satisfied with the price they were getting for their cheese ; for its quantity, and perhaps quality, we were equally sure that the greenness of their meadows was a sufficient guarantee. By the wayside we saw women with baskets full of wormwood, for making absinthe which will be drunk in Paris.

We breakfasted at Lausanne, and dined and slept at Vevey. We had thus got to Switzerland, practically, in no time at all, and without any fatigue, for we had been on the way only at night, and both nights we had managed to get sleep enough.

We had come, as it were, on the magical bit of carpet of Eastern imagination ; which must have been meant for a foreshadowing of that great magician, the locomotive, suggested by a yearning for the annihilation of long journeys, without roads, and with no conveyance better than a camel : though a friend of mine, whose fancy ranges freely and widely through things in heaven above, and on earth below, tells me he believes that that bit of carpet was a dim reminiscence of a very advanced state of things in an old by-gone world, out of some fragments of the wreck of which the existing order of things has slowly grown.

My last hours in London had been spent in dining at the club, with a friend, who is one of our greatest authorities on sanitary, educational, and social questions ; and our talk had been on such subjects. It is well to pass as directly as possible, and without tarrying by the way, from London and Paris, where man, his works, and interests are everything, to Switzerland, where nature is so impressive. The completeness of the contrast heightens the interest felt in each.

Those who give themselves the trouble, and do you the honour, of looking through what you have written, become, in some degree, entitled to know all about the matter. They are in a sort partners in the concern. I will therefore at once communicate to all the members of the firm that I did not go on this little expedition because I felt any of that desire for change by which, in these days, all the world appears to be driven in Jehu-fashion. I have never felt any necessity for this modern nostrum. I do not find that either body or mind wears out because I remain in one place more than twelve months together. I am a great admirer of White of Selborne; and I hope our present Lord Chancellor's new title will lead many people to ask what Selborne is famous for; which perhaps may be the means of bringing more of us to become acquainted with a book which gives so charming a picture of a most charming mind that it may be read with most soothing delight a score of times in one's life (one never tires of a good picture); and which teaches for these days the very useful lesson of how much there is to observe, and interest, and to educate a mind, and to give employment to it, for a whole life, within the boundaries of one's own parish, provided only it be a rural one.

It is true that I have been in every county of England, and in most counties of Scotland, Ireland, and Wales; and some general acquaintance with his own country—which is undoubtedly the most interesting country in the world—ought to an Englishman, if only for the purpose of subsequent comparison, to be the first acquisition of travel; and also that I have made some long journeys beyond the four seas, having set foot on each of the four continents; but I can hardly tell how on any one occasion it happened that I went. It certainly never was from any wish for change. It was only from taking things as they came. And so it was with this little excursion. It was not in the least my idea, nor was it at all of my planning. My wife wished to spend the winter in a more genial climate than that of East Anglia; and it was thought desirable that her little boy should go to a Swiss school, for, at all events, a part of the year, until he should be old enough for an English public school. And so, having been invited to go, I went. My part of the business, with the single exception of a little episode we shall come to in its place, was to be ready to start and to stop when required, and to eat what was set before me; in short, to take the goods a present providence purveyed. I recollect a weather-beaten blue-jacket once telling me—on the roof of the York mail, so all that may be changed now—that the charm of a sailor's life was that he had only to do what he was told, and nothing at all to think about. Of this perhaps obsolete nautical kind of happiness, we housekeeping, business-bound landsmen cannot have much; but a month of such travel comes very near it. And if a man really does want change for the body, together with rest for the mind, here he has them both in perfection. What a delightful oasis would many find such a month in their ordinary lives of inadequately discharged, and too inadequately appreciated, responsibility! This little confidence will, perhaps, while we are starting, convey to the reader a sense of the unreserved and friendly terms on which, I hope, we shall travel together. I regret that, from the nature of the case, in these confidences all the reciprocity must be on one side.

August 29.—Left Vevey by an early train for Sierre. The line passes by Montreux, Villeneuve (where it leaves the eastern extremity of the lake of Geneva), Aigle, Bex, St. Maurice, Martigny, and Sion. At Sierre we took the diligence for Visp. This part of the valley of the Rhone is a long delta, which in the lapse of ages has been formed by the *débris* brought down by the Rhone, and the lateral torrents from the mountains. Much of it is swampy, and full of reeds. Some of this, one cannot but suppose, might be made good serviceable land by cutting channels for the water, and raising the surface of the land with the materials thus gained. Indian corn grows here very luxuriantly. It is a large variety; some of the stems had three cobs. This, the potatoes, and the tobacco—of which, or, at all events, of the smoke of which, we saw much—in thought connected the scene before us with the New World.

Between Sierre and Visp there are a great many large mounds in the valley. The side of these mounds which looks up the valley is always rounded. The face which looks down the valley, is sometimes rocky and precipitous. This difference must be the effect of former glacier action, at a time when the whole valley, down to Geneva, was the bed of a glacier, which planed off and rounded only that side of the mound against which it moved and worked. Above Visp the land is very poor, consisting chiefly of cretaceous detrital matter. This is covered with a pine forest, a great part of which is composed of Scotch fir, the old ones being frequently decorated with tufts of mistletoe.

Geologists are now pretty well agreed that the lake of Geneva itself was excavated by this old glacier. Its power, at all events, was adequate to the task. It was 100 miles long, and near 4,000 feet in thickness at the head of the lake, as can now be seen by the striated markings it left on the overhanging mountains. It acted both as a rasp—its under side being set with teeth, formed of the rocks it had picked up on its way, or which had fallen into it through its crevasses; and also as a scoop, pushing before it all that it could thrust out of its way. And what could not such a tool rasp away and scoop out, at a point where its rasping and scooping were brought into play, as it slid along, thicker than Snowdon is high above the sea, and impelled by the pressure of the 100 miles of descending glacier behind, that then filled the whole broad valley up to and beyond Oberwald? It was wasting away as it approached the site of the modern city, where it must have quite come to an end; for the lake here shoals to nothing; there could, therefore, have, then, been no more rasping and scooping. At the head of the lake, where the glacier-tool was tilted into the position for rasping and scooping vigorously, the water, notwithstanding subsequent detrital depositions, is 900 feet deep.

At Visp my wife and the little boy got on horseback. Another horse was engaged for the baggage. I proceeded on foot. Our destination was Zermatt. We got under weigh at 2 P.M., and reached St. Niklaus at 5.45; about twelve miles of easy walking. The situation of this place is good, for the valley is here narrow, and the mountains, particularly on the western side, rise abruptly. The inn also is good. I note this from a sense of justice, deepened by a sense of gratitude; because here an effort, rare in Swiss hotels, has been made to exclude stenches from the house; the plan adopted being that of a kind of external Amy Robsart gallery. From Visp to St. Niklaus the road is passable only for horses.

August 30.—My wife and the little boy took a *char* for Zermatt, which also carried the baggage. I was on foot. The distance is about fourteen or fifteen miles, slightly up hill all the way. The road is good and smooth. I must now begin to mention the conspicuous objects seen by the way. At Randa, in the Bies Glacier, which is that of the Weisshorn, we saw our first ice. This glacier descends so precipitously from the mountains, on the right of the road, that you can hardly understand how its enormous weight is supported. There are, however, on record some instances of its having fallen; and it is also on record that on one of these occasions the blast of wind caused by the fall of such a mass, was so great as to launch the timbers of houses it overthrew to the distance of a mile; but I would not back the truth of the record.

After an early dinner at Zermatt, my wife and myself walked to the foot of the Gorner Glacier, to see the exit from it of the Visp. It issues from a most regularly arched aperture. This is the glacier that descends from the northern and western sides of Monte Rosa, the sides of the Breithorn, and one side of the mighty Matterhorn.

We found the hotels at Zermatt overcrowded. This is a great rendezvous for those who do peaks and passes. In the evening, particularly if it is cold enough for a fire, the social cigar brings many of them together in the smoking-room. Among these, at the time we were there, was the hero of the season. He is a strong, wiry man, full of quiet determination. He was then doing, so ran the talk of the hotel, a mountain a day, and each in a shorter time than it had ever been done in before. To-morrow he is to climb the Matterhorn in continuous ascent from this place, in which fashion I understand no one has yet attempted it.

CHAPTER II.

THE RIFFEL—THE GORNER GRAT—SUNDAY—ZERMATT—SCHWARTZ SEE—MOUNTAINEERING

> Not vainly did the early Persian make
> His altar the high places, and the peak
> Of earth-o'ergazing mountains ; and thus take
> A fit and unwalled temple, there to seek
> The Spirit, in whose honour shrines are weak,
> Uprear'd of human hands.—BYRON.

August 31.—After breakfast my wife and I walked up to the Riffel Hotel. It is rather more than 3,000 feet above Zermatt. The little man rode. We were two hours and a half in doing it. It would be a stiff bit for beginners. The upper part of the forest, on the mountain-side, consists of Pinus Cembra. This is far from being either a lofty or a spreading tree. The lower branches extend but little beyond the upper ones. There is a good deal of reddish-brown in the bark. In this respect, as well as in the colour of its foliage, and in its form, it contrasts well with the larch and the spruce, though of course not so well with the Scotch fir. I heard that its timber is very lasting.

The views, from the forest, of the Gorner glacier, and, when you are beyond the forest, of some of the neighbouring mountains, and of the valley of Zermatt, are good.

After luncheon at the Riffel Hotel, we walked to the summit of the Gorner Grat. Here you have what is said to be the finest Alpine view in Europe. You are standing on a central eminence of rock in, as far as you can see, a surrounding world of ice and snow. On the left is the Cima di Jazi, which you are told commands a good view into Italy. Just before you, as you look across the glacier, which lies in a deep broad ravine at your feet, rise the jagged summits of Monte Rosa with, at this season, much of the black rock showing through their caps and robes of snow. Next the Lyskamm, somewhat in the background; then Castor and Pollux, immaculate snow without protruding rock; next the Breithorn, then the naked gneiss of the Matterhorn, a prince among peaks, too precipitous for snow to rest on in the late summer, looking like a Titanic Lycian tomb, such as you may see in the plates of 'Fellowes's Asia Minor,' placed on the top of a Titanic rectangular shaft of rock, five thousand feet high. Beyond, and completing the circle of the panorama, come the Dent Blanche, the Gabelhorn, the Rothhorn, the Weisshorn, over the valley of Zermatt, the Ober Rothhorn, and the Allaleinhorn, which brings your eye round again to the Cima di

Jazi. What a scene! what grandeur for the eye! what forces and masses beneath for the thought! Here is the complement to Johnson's Charing Cross and the East Anglican turnip-field. Both pleasant sights in their respective classes, but not enough of all that this world has to show.

The little boy in the morning, during our ascent of the Riffel, had not been able, when he dismounted, to take a dozen steps without resting, as it appeared both from having outgrown his strength, and from some difficulty in breathing; but in the afternoon he skipped up to the top of the Gorner Grat, an hour and a half, and ran down again, just as if he had been bred on the mountains. It was difficult to keep him on the path, and from the edges of the precipices. He was at the top some minutes before any of us— we were a large party, for several parties had drawn together in the ascent. I heard a lady exclaim, 'There is the blue boy again' (that was the colour of his blouse). 'He has beaten us all.' Never was there such a difference before between a morning and an afternoon.

As we descended the Gorner Grat a scud of snow passed by. The antithesis, common in the mountains, of gloom to sunshine, and of cold to warmth, was as complete as it was sudden. In a few minutes it was bright and warm again.

While we were at the hotel two American lads

came up with their guides, and, after a rest of ten minutes, started for some pass. They had nothing on but coarse grey woollen pants, shirts of the same without collars, and boots very heavily nailed, or rather spiked. They were not more than seventeen years old, if so much.

The Riffelberg abounds in beautiful flowers; Gentians, Sedums, and Saxifrages reach almost to the top of the Gorner Grat. As might be expected at such a height, none rise, at their best, more than an inch or two above the ground. Gorgeous lilies and lovely roses would be as much out of keeping, as impossible, here. Such objects belong to the sensuous valley.

September 1.—There was a sharp frost this morning, but the sun was bright and warm all day. So warm was it at ten o'clock, that people were glad to sit about on the grass, some preferring the shade of the rocks. It was Sunday, and I was requested to conduct divine service. The reading saloon was prepared for the purpose. I shortened the service by omitting the first lesson, the *Te Deum*, and the Litany. Before commencing, I announced to the congregation that I should do this, giving as my reason that the room did not belong exclusively to us, and therefore that it was better to act upon our knowledge of this, than to be reminded of it afterwards by those who had withdrawn that we might hold our service. I had been called upon to conduct the service only a few minutes before it commenced, and as I had no memoranda for sermons with me, I took for my text the scene around us, and spoke of the effects such scenes, and the contemplation of nature generally, appear to have on men's minds. The knowledge men now have of the solar system, and of the sidereal universe, does not prevent the heavens from discoursing to us as eloquently as they did to the Psalmist. Intelligible law is grander and more satisfactory for thought to rest upon than vague impressions of glorious power. So with the great and deep sea also, now that we know something about the place it occupies in the economy of this terrestrial system. It is the same with the everlasting mountains, since we have come to know something about the way in which they were formed and elevated, and how the valleys were cut out. Man is the child of Nature, in whose bosom he is brought up. It is true that there are some who cannot see that it is his duty and his happiness to acquaint himself with nature; but no one who had made any progress in the study of nature, ever thought lightly of what he had attained to. And this is true of the knowledge, not only of the grander objects of nature, such as the starry firmament and the great and deep sea, but equally of the most inconspicuous, and, as they appear to our senses, the most insignificant objects in nature. It is not more true of the eternal mountains than of the particles of moss that hide themselves in the crevices of the rock, or the lichen that stains its face, &c., &c.

In the afternoon we walked back to Zermatt.

Though every effort was being made at Zermatt to prevent people from going up to the Riffel without tickets assuring them of accommodation at the Riffel Hotel, still, so many, in their impatience, set this regulation at defiance, and went up on the chance that they would be allowed six feet by three somewhere, that night after night, as we were told, the authorities were obliged—perhaps it was a necessity which was accepted not unwillingly—to convert the bureau, the *salle-à-manger*, and the reading-room, into dormitories. At all events, we were turned out of the reading-room before ten o'clock to make way for a pile of mattresses we found at the door, ready to be substituted for the chairs and tables we had been using. To be berthed in this way is far from pleasant; but it is not worse than spending the night in the crowded cabin of a small steamer, or in the hermetically-closed compartment of a railway carriage, with five other promiscuous bodies.

September 2.—Started this morning for the Schwartz See and Hornli. We were all mounted—it was the only time I was during the excursion. In ascending the mountain, when we were above the pine-wood, and so in a place where there was no protection, and where the zigzags were short and precipitous, both the hind legs of the little boy's horse slipped off the path. The animal was so old, and worn-out, and dead-beaten with its daily drudgery, that it had appeared to us not to care, hardly to know, whether it was dead or alive. But now it made an effort to recover itself, with the power or disposition for making which we should not, beforehand, have credited it. Perhaps the centre of gravity in the poor brute was never actually outside the path. I was close behind, and saw the slip and scramble. It was an affair of a few seconds, but it made one feel badly for more minutes.

At the Schwartz See, we sent the horses to the foot of the Zmutt glacier, and began the ascent of the Hornli. In about a quarter of an hour we made the discovery that the blue boy was not man enough for the Hornli. I do not know, however, that we should have seen much more if we had gone to the top. We were close to the mighty Matterhorn, of which the Hornli is a buttress, and at our feet was the great Gorner glacier. These were the two great objects, and neither of them would have been seen so well had we been higher up. In returning we went by the way of the Zmutt glacier, a wild scene of Alpine desolation. There is much variety, and much that interests in this excursion; the cultivated valley, the junction of the Findelen and the Zmutt with the Visp, the wooded and then the naked mountain, the two great glaciers, the sedgy, flowery turf above

C

the wood, the little black tarn, the bare rock of the Hornji, and, over all, the shaft of the Matterhorn. On the ridge above the Schwartz See we found a handsome blue pansy. Somewhere else I saw a yellow one of almost equal size.

Our guide, Victor Furrer, speaks English well. He wished to come to England for the seven winter months, thinking that he could take the place of under-gardener or stableman in a gentleman's house, or that of porter in a London hotel. Swiss education disposes the people to look for openings for advancing themselves in life beyond the narrow limits of their own country, and qualifies them for entering them.

The number of peak-climbers and pass-men assembled at Zermatt had increased during our short absence. Among the latter was an Irish judge, who did the St. Theodule. The law was in great force here, as was also the Church. The gentleman who had attempted the Matterhorn on Saturday, had been driven off by the weather. Though fine down here, it had been windy, wet, and frosty up there; and to such a degree that the face of this Alpine pier, for it is more of that than of a mountain, had become glazed with a film of ice. To-day he again attempted it from this place; and, the weather having been all that could be desired, he had gone, and climbed, and conquered. He found the air so calm on the summit that he had no occasion to protect the match with which he lighted his cigar; and, if he had had a candle, he would have left it lighted for the people at the Riffel to look at through their telescopes.

Notwithstanding the argument which may be founded on the graves (one a cenotaph) of the four Englishmen in the God's acre of the Catholic church of Zermatt, one cannot but sympathise with the triumph, and applaud the pluck and endurance of our mountaineering countrymen. It must be satisfactory, very satisfactory indeed, for a man to find that he has such undeniable evidence that he is sound in wind and limb, and, too, with a heart and head to match; and that he can go anywhere and do anything, for which these by no means insignificant qualifications are indispensable. Mountaineering, in its motives, to a great extent resembles hunting, and, where there is a difference, the difference is, I think, to its advantage. It is more varied, more continuously exciting, more appreciated by those who do not participate in it, and, which is a great point, more entirely personal, for your horse does not share the credit with you. Shooting and fishing can bear no comparison with it. The pluck, endurance, and manliness it requires are not needed by them. It is also a great merit that it is within the reach of those who have not been born to hunting, fishing, and shooting, and will never have the means of paying for them. All these pursuits have each its own literature; and, as the general public appears to take most interest in that of the mountaineers, there is in this, as far as it goes, reason for supposing that the pursuit itself is of all of them the most rational and stirring.

Alpinism is also a natural and healthy protest in some, whose minds and bodies are young and vigorous, against the dull drawing-room routine of modern luxury; and in others against the equally dull desk-drudgery of semi-intellectual work, to which so many are tied down in this era of great cities. It is for a time a thorough escape from it. It is the best form of athleticism, which has its roots in the same causes; and it is, besides, a great deal which athleticism is not.

To a bystander there is something amusing in the quiet earnestness with which a peak-climber discusses the possibilities of an ascent he is contemplating. I was with two this afternoon who were about to attempt a mountain by a side on which it had not yet been scaled. The difficulty was what had hitherto been regarded as pretty much of a sheer precipice of some hundreds of feet. One of the two, however, had examined it carefully with his glass, and had come to think that there was roughness enough on its face for their purpose. The guides who were present were of the opposite opinion. That it had never been ascended on that side, but might perhaps prove not unascendable, was the attraction.

CHAPTER III.

WALK BACK TO ST. NIKLAUS—AGRICULTURE—LIFE—
RELIGION IN THE VALLEY

> Whate'er men do, or wish, or fear; their griefs
> Distractions, joys.—JUVENAL.

September 3.—Left Zermatt at 2 P.M. on foot. Walked briskly, but did not get to St. Niklaus till near 6 o'clock. All the way down hill. In coming up was only a quarter of an hour longer; this I can't understand. A very warm day. Those who went in *chars*, as did my wife and the blue boy, appeared to suffer more from the heat than I did who was walking.

In my four hours' walk, having been so lately over the same ground, I paid attention to the methods and results of cultivation, and endeavoured to make out something of the life of the inhabitants of the valley. As to the former, it appeared that all the cultivated land had been reclaimed by a slow and laborious process. The original condition of mountain valley land is to be more or less covered with rocks and stones, with some soil beneath and between. Sometimes the whole surface is completely covered with rocky *débris*, which has been brought down, like avalanches, on the occurrence of unusually copious torrent floods, which were, in fact, avalanches of water and of mountain shingle commingled. The first step in the work of reclamation is to get rid of the stones. This is either done by removing them to a distance, or piling them up in heaps, or burying them on the spot. One of these methods will be best in one place, and another in another. All the soil that can be procured—sometimes there is enough of it on the surface, sometimes it has to be mined for in a stratum beneath the upper stratum of fragments of rock—is then levelled. Of this land, thus laboriously made, all that can be irrigated by lateral canals brought from the Visp, or diverted from the mountain torrents, is laid down to pasture. Canals of this kind may often be seen some miles in length. These irrigated pastures are always cut twice, or, where the land is deep and good, three times a year. The turf is not always composed mainly of different kinds of grass. Sometimes it contains more dandelion than grass, a great abundance of autumn crocus, of a kind of geranium with a purple flower as large as a florin, and of other herbaceous plants. Where there is much dandelion the hay, while making, has a sickly smell, but when fully made its scent is generally good. The reclaimed land, which cannot be irrigated, is used for rye, wheat, barley, and potatoes. A well-to-do family has two or three patches, about a third of an acre each, of this grain land. They will have also two or three cows. The mountain forest, and the mountain pastures are held in common for the equal use and benefit of all the inhabitants of the village.

As to the people themselves, the most prominent facts are that they all work hard, and that their hard work does not give them more than a bare sufficiency for the most necessary wants. I suppose that nowhere else in the civilised world is there so little buying and selling, and so little interchange of commodities, as in a Swiss Alpine valley. The rule is for every family to be self-contained, as far as this is possible, in all things, and to produce for itself everything it can of what it will require in the twelve months. Their cows supply them with milk and cheese; the surplus of the latter being the medium through which they procure from the outside world what they cannot produce for themselves: but that does not come to much. It is interesting to see their sheaves of corn stored away in the galleries beneath the projecting eaves of their houses, and their haricots strung up in the sun to dry. This makes you think how carefully these provisions will be used in the winter and spring. And you see the flax and the hemp, of which they grow a great deal, spread out on the grass, to prepare it for scutching; from which, and from the wool of the small flocks of the neighbourhood, they make at home much of the materials for their clothes. From their apples, of which they grow great quantities, they make a kind of brandy. Their lives are a never-failing discipline, notwithstanding the brandy, of industry, patience, and forethought. In imagination you enter the *châlet*, and sympathise with the cares, the troubles, the frugality, the modest enjoyments of its inmates. The result of all does not go much beyond daily bread. You hope that the harvest has been good, and that the cows are doing well. The boys you have seen are sturdy little fellows. You hope that the girls will not be goitred, and that the sturdy little fellows will in time make them good husbands. They, you are sure, will make industrious, frugal, uncomplaining wives.

We heard at Zermatt, and our guide told us that what we had heard was true, that the inhabitants of the valley pass some of their time in winter in playing at cards; the stake they play for being each other's prayers. Those who lose are bound by the rules of the game to go to the village church the following morning, and there pray for the souls of those who win. The priest also is supposed to have an advantage in this practice, as it gives him a larger congregation.

Religion—the reader will decide for himself whether or no what has just been mentioned promotes it—holds a large place in the life of these Alpine valleys. The priest is the great man of the village, and has great power. The influx of travellers has a tendency to lessen this power, for it enriches inn-keepers and guides, and so renders them independent. Formerly the village church was the only conspicuous building; the only one that rose above the low level of the *châlets*. This symbolised the relation of its minister to the inhabitants of the *châlets*. Now the church is dwarfed in comparison with the contiguous hotel. Changes in the world outside have caused a new power to spring up, and take its place in the scene. Be this, however, as it may, one cannot but see that the services and *fêtes* of the Church, supply the hard monotonous lives of the people with some ideas and interest. Even the authority the Church claims, while it has a tendency to overpower, has also a tendency to stir their minds a little. The prominence of the material fabric of the church in the village led me to reflect on what would be the result in the minds of the people if it were otherwise. In that case they would probably lose the idea of union with other times, and with the great outside world, and the little elevation of thought and feeling beyond the round of their low daily cares, which that idea brings with it. The Church may to them be an intellectual tyranny, and much that it teaches may be debasing and false, still it appears to have some counterbalancing advantages. Our system may have more of truth and of manliness, but it would, at present, be unintelligible to them, or if intelligible, repulsive. Their system, however, is one which, under the circumstances of the times, cannot last. It is even now on the road to the limbo of things that have had their day. In Catholic countries, as far as the educated classes and the inhabitants of all the large cities are concerned, its power is gone, or still more than that, it is actively disliked. This settles the question. The time will arrive when, as knowledge and light spread, the village people will come round to the way of thinking of the educated classes and of the inhabitants of the cities. In this matter history is repeating itself. At its first establishment Christianity spread from the cities to the pagans, that is to the inhabitants of the villages. And so will it be again, at the rehabilitation of religion in those countries that are now forsaking Romanism. A revised and enlarged organisation of knowledge must be first accepted by those who can think and judge. It is then passed on to those who cannot.

Such valleys as this of Zermatt have hitherto offered no opportunities to any portion of their inhabitants to emerge from a low condition of life. Little that could elevate or embellish life was within their reach. The only property has been land, and that, from the working of inevitable natural causes, has been divided into very small holdings. This has kept every family poor. Railways, which connect them with the world, the influx of travellers, in many places a better harvest than that of their fields, the advance of the rest of the world around them, and the capacity there is in their streams for moving machinery, may be now opening new careers to many. It is unreasonable to regret the advent of such a change, for it has more than a material side; it must bring with it, morally and intellectually, a higher and richer life. It implies expansion of mind, and moral growth—new fields of thought, and of duty.

CHAPTER IV.

I. PEASANT-PROPRIETORSHIP IN THE VALLEY. II. LANDLORDISM. III. THE ERA OF CAPITAL. IV. OBSTRUCTIONS TO THE FREE INTERACTION OF CAPITAL AND LAND —THEIR EFFECTS, AND PROBABLE REMOVAL. V. CO-OPERATIVE FARMING NOT A STEP FORWARDS

> But what said Jaques?
> Did he not moralise the spectacle?—SHAKESPEARE.

THIS chapter is to be a disquisition, after the manner of the philosophers, at all events, in its length, on peasant-proprietorship as now existing in the valley of Zermatt, or rather of the Visp; and on alternative systems. I do not invite anyone to read it, indeed, I at once announce its contents and its length, for the very purpose of inducing those who have no liking for disquisitions in general, or for disquisitions on such subjects, to skip it, and to proceed to the next chapter, where they will find the continuation of the narrative of our little excursion. My primary object in writing it was to ascertain, through the test of black and white, whether what I had been led to think upon these matters possessed sufficient coherence. I now, with the diffidence one must feel who ventures upon such ground, submit it to the judgment of those who take some interest in questions of this kind.

Bearing in mind that the subject is not a lively one, I will endeavour so to put what I have to say as that not much effort may be required to understand my meaning. From all effort, however, I cannot exempt the reader of the chapter, should it find one; for he will have, as he goes along, to determine for himself whether the facts alleged are the facts of the case, whether any material ones have been overlooked, and whether the inferences are drawn from the facts legitimately. He will not be in a position to allow what is presented to him to pass unquestioned; for he will be, himself, the counsel on the other side, as well as the jury.

I. The figures I am about to use do not pretend to accuracy, or even to any close approximation to accuracy. Some figures, but what figures is of no great consequence, are necessary for the form of the argument, and for rendering it intelligible. If they possessed the most precise accuracy that would not at all strengthen it. Those I employ, I retain merely because they were the symbols with which, in my two walks through the valley, I endeavoured to work out the inquiry.

Suppose, then, that the valley of the Visp contains 4,000 acres of irrigated meadow and of corn and garden ground ; and that each family is composed of husband and wife, and of not quite four children. The average here in England is, I believe, four and a half children to a marriage. Marriages, probably, take place at a later period of life in the valley than in this country, and, therefore, the average number of children there will be smaller. Let, then, the grandfathers and grandmothers who may be living, and the unmarried people there may be, bring up the average of each family to six souls.

We will now suppose that the husband will require a pound and a half of bread a day, that will be about nine bushels of wheat a year; and that the wife and children will require each a pound a day ; that will be about thirty bushels more, or thirty-nine bushels in all. From what I saw of the land in the valley I suppose that it will not produce more than twenty-six bushels an acre. Whether its produce be wheat, or rye, or barley, will make no difference to the argument. An acre and a half will then be necessary for the amount of bread-stuff that will be required for each family.

A family, we will take a well-to-do one, will also require three cows. Deducting the time the cows are on the common pasture on the mountains, each cow will require, for the rest of the year, two tons of hay. That may be the produce of one acre of their grassland, for some of it is cut three times a year, but most of it only twice, the second and third crops being light.

They will not want for their own consumption the whole of the produce of the three cows. A surplus, however, of this produce is necessary, because it is from that that they will have the means for purchasing the shoes, the tools and implements, and whatever else they absolutely need, but cannot produce themselves. The cows will then require three acres.

But we will suppose that by the use of straw, and by other economies in the keep of their cows, they manage to reduce the quantity of hay that would otherwise be consumed. This will set free a little of their land for flax, hemp, haricots, cabbages, potatoes, &c. The three last will go some way towards lessening the quantity of bread-stuff they will require. We may, therefore, set down the breadth of cultivated land needed for the maintenance, according to their way of living, of our family of six souls, at four acres.

The 4,000 acres will thus maintain 1,000 families. This will give our valley a population of 6,000 souls.

Here, perhaps, the rigid economist would stop. It would be enough for him to have ascertained the laws which regulate, under observed circumstances, the production and the distribution of wealth. But as neither the writer nor the readers of these pages are rigid economists, we will, using these facts only as a starting point, proceed to ulterior considerations. The question, indeed, which most interests us is not one of pure economy, but one which, though dependent on economical conditions, is in itself moral and intellectual; and, therefore, we go on to ask what kind of life, what kind of men and women, does this state of things produce?

In such a population, the elements of life are so simple, so uniform, and so much on the surface, that there will be no difficulty in getting at the answers to our questions. There is not a single family that has the leisure needed for mental cultivation, or for any approximation to the embellishments of life. They each have just the amount of land which will enable them, with incessant labour, and much care and forethought, to keep themselves above absolute want. Subdivision might, possibly, in some cases be carried a little further, but things would then only become worse. Towards this there is always a tendency. But, for reasons we shall come to presently, there is no tendency at all in the other direction. Intellectual life, therefore, is impossible in the valley. The conditions requisite for it are completely absent.

With the moral life, however, it is very far from being so. Of moral educators, one of the most efficient is the possession of property; the kind of education it gives being, of course, dependent on the amount and kind of property. For instance: the simplicity and gentility of a large fortune in three per cent. consols educates its possessor. It does not teach him forethought, industry, or self-denial. He may be improvident, idle, self-indulgent, and still his means of living may not be thereby diminished; nor will anything he can do improve them. Nor, furthermore, will the management of his property bring him into such relations with his fellow men, that, at every step and turn, he has to consider their wants and rights, and to balance them against his own. Nor will anything connected with his property teach him the instability of human affairs, for his is just the only human possession that is exempt from all risks and changes. Now the non-teaching of these moral qualities is an education, the outcome of which is likely to be a refined selfishness. An equal fortune derived from commerce, trade, or manufactures, teaches other lessons, almost we may say lessons of the very opposite kind. He, whose position depends on buying and selling, and producing, and on the human agencies he must make use of, on new discoveries, and on a variety of natural occurrences, will estimate life and his fellow men very differently from his neighbour, who has nothing at all to do except receiving, and spending his dividends. We are taking no account of individual character, and of the thousand circumstances and accidents, which may overrule, in any particular case, the natural teaching of either of these two kinds of property: we are only speaking generally; and are taking them as illustrations, with which we are all familiar, of a character-forming power every kind of property possesses.

Looking, then, at the property possessed by these Visp-side families in the same way, we can readily understand the moral effect it will have upon them. It will enforce what it teaches with irresistible power, because it will be acting on every member of the community in precisely the same way, throughout every day of the lives of all of them, generation after generation. Such teaching there is no possibility of withstanding. And what it teaches in this undeniable fashion,—undeniable because the virtues taught are to them the very conditions of existence,—are very far from being small moralities, for they are industry, prudence, patience, frugality, honesty.

Without industry their little plots of land could not support them; not the industry of the Irishman, in the days before the potato-famine, who set his potatoes in the spring, and took them up in the autumn, without finding much to do for the rest of the year; but an industry which must be exercised, sometimes under very adverse circumstances, throughout the whole twelve months. Every square yard of every part of their land represents so much hard labour, for nowhere has land been so hard to win. This fact is always before their eyes, and is in itself always a lesson to them. And this hard-won land, reminding them of the industry of those who were before them, has still, always, to be protected against the ravages of winter storms, and its irrigation kept in order. And every hard-won square yard must be turned to the best account. And all must labour in doing this. Their cows, too, require as much attention as their families. For them they must toil unremittingly in their short summer: they must follow them up into the mountains, and they must collect and store up for them the provender they will need in the long winter. And they must be industrious not only in the field, but equally in the house. They cannot afford to buy, and, therefore, everything, that can be, must be done, and made, at home. They cannot allow any portion of their time, or any capacity their land has for producing anything useful, to run to waste. There can be no fallows, of any kind, here.

With their long winters and scanty means, frugality, prudence, forethought, are all as necessary as industry. These are the indispensable conditions for eking out the consumption of the modest store of necessaries their life-long industry provides. If they were as wasteful, as careless, as improvident as our wages-supported poor, the ibex and chamois might soon return to the valley.

It is these necessity-imposed virtues which save

the valley on the one hand from depopulation, and on the other from becoming overpeopled. Our labourers, and artisans, and operatives, who depend on wages, as soon as they have got wages enough to support a wife, marry. The general, almost the universal, rule with them is to marry young. The young men and maidens on Visp-side, not being dependent on wages, but on having a little bit of land, sufficient to support life, do not marry till they have come into possession of this little bit of land. Early marriages, therefore, are not the rule with them. The discipline of life, such as it is in the valley, has taught them—and a very valuable lesson it is—to bide their time.

Another virtue, which comes naturally to them, is honesty. The honesty of the valley appears to an Englishman unaccountable, Arcadian, fabulous. The ripe apples and the ripe plums hang over the road without a fence, for land is too precious for fences, and within reach of the hand of the passer-by; but no hand is reached out to touch them. Why is such forbearance unimaginable here? The reason is that, where only a few possess, the many not having the instincts of property, come to regard the property of the few as, to some extent, fair game for them. It is their only chance—their only hunting-ground. This is a way in which, without sanctioning a law which will act prejudicially to themselves, they can secure their share of the plums and apples nature provides.

But, when all have property, each sees that the condition on which his own plums and apples will be respected is that he should himself respect the plums and apples of other people. This idea is at work in everybody's mind. The children take to the idea, and to the practice of it, as naturally as they did to their mother's milk. Honesty becomes an element of the general morality. It is in the air, which all must breathe.

Here then is a picture that is most charming. How cruelly hard has Nature been! Look at the cold, heartless mountains. Look upon their ice and storm-engendering heights. See how the little valley below lies at their mercy. Consider how, year by year, they fight against its being extorted from their dominion. Yet the feeble community in the valley, by their stout hearts and virtuous lives, continue to make it smile on the frowning mountains. How pleasing to the eye and to the thought, is the sight! And what enhances the charm it possesses is the sense of its thorough naturalness. There is nothing artificial about it; and so there is nothing that can to the people themselves suggest discontent. Their condition, in every particular, is the direct result of the unobstructed working of natural causes, such as they exist in man himself, and in environing circumstances. Whatever may be its drawbacks, or insufficiencies, they can in no way be traced to human legislation. How unwilling are we to contrast with this charming scene—but this is just what we have to do—the destitution, the squalor, and the vice, not of our great cities only, but even of our Visp-sides.

But, first, we will endeavour, by the light of the ideas we outside people have on these subjects, to complete our estimate of the worth of the state of things we are contemplating; of this oasis, the sight of which is so refreshing to those whose lot it is to be familiar with, and to dwell in, the hard wilderness of the world.

Its virtues are, doubtless, very pleasing to contemplate; but they are not of quite the highest order. The industry before us is very honourable. The mind dwells on the sight of it with satisfaction. But, as it only issues in the barest subsistence, the observation of this somewhat clouds our satisfaction. There are, too, higher forms of industry of which nothing can be known here—the industry of those who live laborious days, and scorn delights, from the desire to improve man's estate, to extort the secrets of nature for his benefit, to clear away obstacles which are hindering men from seeing the truth, to add to the intellectual wealth of the race, to smoothe the path of virtue, and make virtue itself appear more attractive. Such industry is more honourable, and more blessed both to him who labours and to those who participate in the fruits of his labour. And such prudence, frugality, and forethought as are practised in the valley are very honourable, and the mind dwells on the sight of them, too, with satisfaction. But he who belongs to the outside world will here again be disposed to repeat the observation just made. It is true that that man's understanding and heart must be out of harmony with the conditions of this life, and therefore repulsive to us, who does not gather up the fragments that nothing be lost, but when this is done only for self, and those who are to us as ourselves, though so done unavoidably through the necessity of the case, it is somewhat chilling and hardening. And it is not satisfactory that so much thought and care should be expended only upon the best use of the means of life—those means, too, being sadly restricted; for a higher application of these virtues would be to the best use of life itself. And so, again, with respect to their honesty. This is a virtue that is as rare as honourable; and the mind dwells on the sight of it with proportionate satisfaction. But its application to plums and apples is only its beginning. It has far loftier and more arduous, and more highly rewarded forms. It may be acted on under difficulties, and applied to matters, not dreamt of in the valley. It may rise into the form of social and political justice, in which form it prompts a man to consider the rights of others, especially of the most helpless and depressed, and even of the vicious, as well as his own; and not to use his own advantages and power in such a way as to hurt or hinder them: but, rather, to consider that it is due to their unhappy circumstances and weakness, that he should so use his power, and good fortune, as to contribute to the redress of the evils of their ill fortune.

Attractive, then, as is the contemplation of the moral life of the inhabitants of the valley, it is not in every respect satisfactory. A higher level may be attained. After all, it is the moral life rather of an ant-hill, or of a bee-hive, than of this rich and complex world to which we belong. And even if it were somewhat more elevated than it is, still there would remain some who would be unable to accept it, as worthy of being retained without prospect of change or improvement; and their reason would be, that man does not live by, or for, morality only. The worthy exercise of the intellectual powers is necessary for their idea of the complete man; and here everything of this kind is found to be sorely deficient. On the whole, then, in respect of each of the three ingredients of human well-being, a thoroughly equipped life, intellectual activity, and the highest form of virtue, we feel that something better,—with respect, indeed, to the two first something very much better,—is attainable, than what exists in the charming oasis before us.

II. I now invite the reader to proceed with me to the consideration of how different economical conditions, such as our experience enables us to imagine, would modify the state of things we have been contemplating. For instance, suppose Visp-side were in Scotland or England, then its 4,000 acres might, and it is not unlikely that they would, be only a part of the estate of some great landlord. Let us endeavour to make out the effects this would have on its inhabitants.

The most obvious result would be that the population would be diminished by more than a half. At present the produce of the valley, with no very considerable deductions, is consumed in the valley. What is produced is what is required for supplying its large population with the first wants of life. But this will no longer be the case. The land will be let. We will suppose that this change has been completely effected; and that its irrigated meadows, with the contiguous little plots of corn-land, have been formed into farms, and that all is now treated in the way those who rent them find it pays best to manage them. We will suppose they have to pay a rent of 30s. an acre. The rent of the valley will then be 6,000*l.* a-year. How will this sum be made up? Cheese, of course, will be the main means. The young bullocks and the old cows will come next. We will take little credit for corn or potatoes, because it is evident that not nearly so much of them will be grown as was done under the old system; for much of the mountain corn-land will not pay now for cultivation with hired labour.

The economist, pure and simple, may say that this is all right. The course of events must be submitted to. Whatever they dictate is best; and best as it is. Interference with natural laws is always bad. The cheese and the cattle will sell for as much as they are worth. The sovereigns they will fetch are worth as much as the produce. There will be no diminution of wealth. But, however, it has to be proved that the new system is unavoidable in the sense of being either a natural step in the unobstructed course of human affairs, or, as some would tell us, the natural consummation of their long course, now at last happily effected. Perhaps it may be possible to show that there has been serious interference with their natural evolution; so serious as greatly to affect their character. And, if so, then the question of whether or no there has been any loss of value does not arise, for the antecedent question may render its discussion unnecessary. Be, however, these matters as they may, they do not cover all the ground we are desirous of investigating. We are thinking not of exchangeable wealth only, but also of men and women; and they, perhaps, may be regarded as wealth in its highest form; a kind of wealth, in which, if the men and women are not corrupt or counterfeit, but good and true, all may to some extent participate, and be the better for.

Under the system we are now considering, it jars against a sense of something or other in the minds of many, to see so much of the results of the labour of the people of the valley passing away from them, never to return in any form or degree. As far as they are concerned it is a tribute they are paying to the man who owns the land of the valley. And whether it be, year by year, paid to him, or whether all this cheese and all these cattle be every year on a stated day collected and burnt at the mouth of the valley; or the price, for which they may have been sold, thrown into the mid-ocean, would make no difference to them. They will get no advantage from it at all, for it is evident that a man who has an income of at least 6,000*l.* a-year will never live in the Valley of the Visp. He will, perhaps, have his mansion on the bank of the Lake of Geneva; or perhaps at Paris: at all events, it will be somewhere at a distance. The case of so many bales of calico being sent out of Manchester, to all parts of the world, is not similar. They are sent out for the very purpose of coming back again in the form of what will not only support those who produce them, but will also, if trade be good, increase the fund that supports the trade, that is to say, will increase the number of those who in various ways are supported by the trade : hence the growth of Manchester. Nor is it the same thing as so many quarters of corn being sent from America to this country, for in that case also the price of the corn returns to the hands of those who grew it. Their corn-fields have produced for them, only in a roundabout fashion, a golden harvest ; and they have, themselves, the consumption of this harvest, precisely in the same way as the now existing Visp-side population have the direct consumption of the produce of their little plots of land. Some, of course, of the price of the cheese and cattle sent away will enable the farmers to live and to pay their labourers ; but none of the 6,000*l*. a-year will come back in any form.

But the point now actually before us is the effect this change will produce on the amount of population. In order that the land might be let profitably, it was necessary to clear it of its old proprietors, for they could pay no rent at all. Their little estates were barely sufficient, with the most unremitting labour, and the most careful frugality, to support life. The valley has now been formed into cheese-farms ; and we will suppose that for keeping up the irrigation, cutting the grass, tending the cows in summer on the mountains, and during the winter doing everything for them, and for cultivating whatever amount of land is still cropped with corn and potatoes, five men are wanted for a hundred acres. This will give for the 4,000 acres 200 men. Let each man, as before, represent a family of six souls. Here, for the labourers and their families, will be a population of 1,200. We will also suppose that, under the circumstances of the valley, the average size of the farms is not more than fifty acres. This will give eighty farmers. If their households average eight souls, we have 640 more. These, and the labourers, will not, as was formerly done, under the old order of things, by every family, produce themselves pretty nearly all that is necessary for their households. It will not be so, because the farmers, who must also attend to their farms, will require many things that none required before; and because the labourers, having to give all their time and strength for wages, will be obliged to buy almost all that they will require. This will necessitate the introduction into the valley of a considerable number of tradesmen. We will suppose a hamlet every five miles, in which, besides farmers and labourers, will reside eight tradesmen and petty shopkeepers. That is five hamlets, and forty tradesmen and shopkeepers. These, with six to a family, will add 240 to the population. These different contributories, then, will raise the total to 2,080. As the distances will remain what they were, and as there will be more stir and ambition among a population of farmers and shopkeepers, than there was formerly among the peasant proprietors, we will take the number of school-teachers as much the same under either system. The reduction of the population to one-third of its former amount will somewhat reduce the number of priests; but as thought will now be more active, and, therefore, more varied, this reduction will be counterbalanced by an increase in the number of prophets.

The next step in our inquiry is, how will this revolution affect the character of the population of the valley? We have seen that under the old system their whole character was the direct result of the fact that everyone was either the actual, or the prospective, possessor of a small plot of land, just enough to sustain the life of a family. That was the root out of which their lives grew; and their industry, frugality, forethought, patience, and honesty were the fruits such lives as theirs produced. That root is now dead. The conditions of life are different; and with different conditions have come corresponding differences of character. For instance, we all know that those who labour primarily for others, that others may make the profit that will accrue from their labour, are not so industrious as those who labour entirely for themselves. Nor will they have the same forethought, because their dependence is on wages, and wages require no forethought. Formerly forethought was a condition of existence. They are also now in a school which is a bad one for frugality and patience, and which is very far from being a good one for honesty. These, however, are still the main constituents of morality, for in them there can be no change, because morality is the regulative order of the family and of society : and now, with respect to all of these points, among the mass of the population, there is, necessarily a deterioration. Nor is petty trade, at least so says the experience of mankind, favourable to morality. As to those who hire the land, we will suppose that the more varied relations, than any which existed under the old system, into which they have been brought with their neighbours, and with the world outside the valley, have in some cases had an elevating and improving effect. The moral influences, however, of occupations of this kind are far from being universally good, because those who live by the labour of others, will in many cases be of opinion, that their own interests are antagonistic to the interests of those they employ in such a sense, that it is to their advantage to pay low wages, which means to lessen the comforts, and even the supply of necessaries, to those by whose labour they live. This may be an unavoidable incident of the relation in which the two stand towards each other, but it is not conducive to the result we are now wishing to find.

The intellectual gains and losses are harder to estimate. As to the labourers, one cannot believe that a body of men that has been lowered morally has been raised intellectually. Among the tradesmen class there will be some who will have more favourable opportunities for rising into a higher intellectual life than any had among the old peasant-proprietors. And among the small occupiers of land, for the farms only average fifty acres, these chances will, perhaps, be still greater. But all this will not come to much. The great question here is about the one family, for whose benefit mainly, almost, indeed, exclusively, the whole of the change has been brought about. This family now stands for 4,000 of the old inhabitants of the valley. One of the greatest of all possible revolutions has been carried out in its favour, for it is a revolution that has swept away the greater part of the population, and completely altered the material, moral, and intellectual life of all that remained. We will, however, suppose that they are everything that can be expected of a family so favourably circumstanced. That their morality is pure and elevated. That, intellectually, they are refined and cultivated. That they promote art. That science is at times their debtor. That among its members have been men who have advanced the thought of their day, and have made additions to the common fund of intellectual wealth ; and others who have done their country good service in peace and in war.

When I say that this family stands in the place of the 4,000 who have disappeared from the valley, I limit the observation to the valley, for I do not mean that the population of the world has been diminished to that extent to make space for them, because the cheese and cattle sent out of the valley for their 6,000*l.* a-year, will contribute to the support elsewhere of a great many people who must work, and so live, in order that they may be able to purchase them.

But to return; those who were not satisfied with the original Arcadian state of things, we may be sure will not be satisfied with that which we are now imagining has taken its place. For nothing will satisfy them, if there must be a change, except some such condition of things as will work as favourably both for morality, and for intellect, as that did for morality alone; and which will, at the same time, provide, generally, a better supplied material life than that did.

We have now endeavoured, first, to analyze the land-system of the valley, such as it presents itself to the eye of a contemplative pedestrian; and which may be regarded as the natural working out of proprietorship in land, when it is the sole means of supporting life. We then proceeded to compare with this a system we wot of, carried out to its full-blown development. This second system is what people refer to when they talk of English landlordism. These two forms, however, of the distribution and tenure of land are very far from exhausting all that have existed, and that do and that might exist. Distribution and tenure are capable of assuming many other forms; and some of these must be considered before we can hope to arrive at anything like a right and serviceable understanding of the matter.

III. The distinguishing feature of the economical conditions of the present day, and of other conditions as far as they depend on those that are economical, is the existence of capital in the forms and proportions it has now assumed. This has modified, and is modifying, the life of all civilised communities. It is this that has built our great cities, that is peopling the new world, that has liberated the serfs of the Russian Empire. It leavens all we do, or say, or think. We are what we are, because of it. The tenure and distribution of land, next to capital itself, the most generally used and diffused of all property, originally the only, and till recently the chief, property, cannot escape the influence of this all-pervading and omnipotent agent of change, which everywhere cuts a channel for itself, and finds the means for rising, sooner or later, to its own level. In some places it has affected land in a fashion more or less in accordance with its natural action; in other places in a fashion which has resulted more or less from artificial restrictions: but in some fashion or other it affects it everywhere ; as it does all man's belongings, and the whole tenor and complexion of human life.

Land, then, was the sole primeval means of supporting life. Over large areas of the earth's surface it is so still. It was so in Homeric Greece—at that time the most advanced part of Europe—though we can trace in its then condition a certain indefinite nebulous capacity for the development of capital, the higher means of supporting life; and which capacity afterwards assumed its true form and action among the Ionians and other Asiatic Greeks, but above all at Athens : which accounts for the differences between it and Sparta : for it was the existence and employment of capital which made it the nurse and the holy city of intellect ; while it was the contempt and the legislative suppression of capital which kept the Lacedæmonians, except so far as they were affected by the general influences of Greek thought, in the condition of a clan of splendid savages. And what obtained all but absolutely in Homeric Greece, obtained at that time, as far as we know, quite absolutely over all the rest of Europe. In the early ages of Roman history, Rome was a city of landowners ; that is, of landowners living a city life. To understand this fact is to understand its early, and much of its subsequent history. It was so, also, with the neighbouring cities, in the conquest and absorption of which the first centuries of its historic existence were spent :

they were cities of landowners. As we walk about the streets of disinterred Pompeii, we see that in this pleasure-city, even down to the late date of its catastrophe, it was very much so, although the capital of the plundered world had, at that time, for several generations, been flowing, through many channels, into Italy. That specimen city, as we may call it, of imperial Italy, appears to have been laid up in its envelope of ashes, preserved like an anatomical preparation, for the very purpose of enabling us to understand this luciferous fact.

I need not go on tracing out the subsequent history of land and capital, which would lead, again, to a comparison of the splendid savagery of feudal landowners with the revival of culture in the capital-supported trading communities of the Dark Ages; and their interaction upon each other: but will pass at once to ourselves. It is very possible now, at all events it is conceivable under the present state of things, that in a large English city—it is more or less so with almost all our cities—there may not be a single owner of agricultural land in its whole population: for I now, as I do throughout this chapter, distinguish land held for agricultural purposes from that which is held merely for residential, or commercial purposes. Here, then, is a difference so great that it takes much time and thought to comprehend its extent, its completeness, and its consequences.

It belongs to a totally different stage of economical, and of social development; as complete as the difference between a caterpillar and a butterfly. The solid strength, the slow movements, the monotonous existence of the former represent the era of land. The nimbleness (capital is of no country), the beauty, the variety of life, but withal the want of solidity of the latter represent the era of capital. It is the wise combination, and harmonious interaction, of the two, which would, and which are destined to, cancel the disadvantages, and secure the advantages of each.

The revolution, that has been effected, is mighty and all-pervading. But because it has not been carried out by invading hosts, ravaged provinces, blazing cities, and bloody battle-fields, it is difficult to bring home to the general understanding that there has been any revolution at all. At its commencement it found those who owned the land of the country, not merely the most powerful order in the state, but quite supreme. It gradually introduced another order of men, those who own capital; and has ended by making them at length the most powerful; and so much so that now, whenever they choose to assert their power, they are supreme. Of course there ought not to be any antagonism between the two; but as there is unfortunately, and quite unnecessarily, an artificially created antagonism, there must be collisions and conflicts; in which, however, the supremacy must always eventually rest with the strongest.

The progress of this revolution ought to be seen a little in detail. Not an acre can be added to the land of the country, but to the capital of the country, already several times as much in value as the whole of the land, and supporting a greater number of lives, there is added a sum of two millions and a half of pounds sterling every Saturday night. We will note a few of the steps in the growth of capital. The year 1550 is very far from the date of the recognised appearance of capital in this country: it was even observed that in the previous century there had been an unexampled extension of commerce; but there are good reasons for supposing that the whole of the accumulated capital of the country at that time was less than one year's purchase of the land. The land, at all events, was worth a great many times as much as all the capital amounted to.

In 1690 the purchase of an estate, of the value of 100,000*l.*, was the wonder of the day.

In the next fifty years bankers were the chief, or only, large purchasers.

In the following half-century the Indians came home, and were added to the class.

Then, in the last half of the last century, came the manufacturers.

And now the most prominent capitalists, who

become large purchasers of land, are the coal-owners, and the owners of iron-works, who, however, are accompanied by a cloud of contractors, engineers, merchants, brewers, Stock Exchange speculators, Australians, and even tradesmen, among whom bankers and manufacturers still hold their ground. Of course all of these classes who might, do not, become purchasers of agricultural estates; but those who do, show us in what direction we are to look for the great money-lords of the day. And if they are so many—there probably are at this time in Newcastle alone, in consequence, just now, of the prosperity of the iron and coal trades, five and twenty houses making, each, its 100,000*l.* a-year, how many must be the rank and file of the army of capital. The ratio then of capital to land has been completely inverted. At this moment there is disposable capital enough in the country to buy, at its present enhanced price, all the land of the country, three times over. And this stock of capital goes on increasing at the rate of 150,000,000*l.* a-year.

In the political order, we are indebted to capital for Sir Robert Peel and Mr. Gladstone, and for their policy; and we may suppose that the policy which capital may dictate will, henceforth, be the policy of every Government that will administer the affairs of this country. The land and the proletariat will never combine for the purpose of attempting to make it otherwise: for it will never be their interest to do so. Capital is both aristocratic and democratic in the best sense of each of these words. It is the cement, and the mainspring of modern societies, and, also, the ladder within them, without which there would be no rising from low to high positions.

And now let us go back to Visp-side, bearing in mind the ideas we have been working out. We will, then, suppose that by trade, and commerce, and manufactures, which are both the children and the parents of capital, other means for supporting life have become abundant in the valley. It is easy to make out what will be the effect of this on the dimensions of the, at present, diminutive properties of its one thousand families. Land will present itself to the minds of all as what it has really become; that is to say, as only one means among many for the support of life: the many others being the various forms in which capital works. The present subdivision, therefore, of the land will no longer be regarded as an obvious and undeniable necessity. It has, indeed, become only a secondary, and inferior means for supporting life. Those engaged in trade and commerce, it will be manifest, are many of them living much better lives than the petty proprietors. The old ideas and practices, then, with respect to land will melt away, and be utterly dissolved. The necessity for maintaining them has ceased; and they will cease to be maintained.

At the same time those who have acquired capital by trade, and commerce, and manufactures, will be desirous of investing some of it, perhaps a surplus their business may not require, in land, which must always continue to be the safest, and in some other respects the most desirable form of property. And many of those who have come to wish to retire from the labours and anxieties of business, will have the same desire. So, too, will some who are disposed to prefer agriculture to other kinds of industry; and who are, therefore, desirous of becoming possessed of sufficient land for their purpose, that they may apply to it their capital and intelligence, using it as the raw material of the manufacture towards which they are most attracted. Some will merely want a pleasant situation for a home for their families; some a little land around such a home to give them a little pleasant occupation. There will, we will suppose, be no artificial, as there are no natural, obstacles to all of these people buying what they have the means for buying, and the wish to buy; and using what they buy as they please. The properties thus formed will, many of them, be large, in proportion to the amount of surplus capital many will come to possess. But what will be remarkable, in this respect, will be, while the number of landed properties will be very considerable, the variety of their dimensions, which will be proportionate to the endlessly varying means of the multitudes, who in an era of capital will be desirous of investing in land, and the variety of uses to which they will be put in accordance with the varying wants and tastes of their owners.

And in these properties, whether great, or small, there will be incessantly at work two directly opposite tendencies. One in the direction of enlargement by inheritance, by marriage, and by larger increases of surplus capital, and of capital retiring from business. The other in the direction of subdivision, through the necessities, or the wishes, of their holders. These necessities may have arisen from the vicissitudes of business, the occurrences of life, and the extravagances and vices of their holders from time to time. Or the descendant of a purchaser may wish to capitalise his land, and take the capital back to business; or to place it in some investment more profitable than land. But, at all events, there will be no escaping from the natural, ever-felt, imperious obligation proprietors of land, like all other men, will be under, of providing for their widows and children. This will keep every estate in the condition of liability to subdivision; and must, at intervals, subdivide it. All these may be regarded as natural conditions. They are self-acting, and never-failing; and that they should lead to their natural issue, that is to the subdivision of landed estates, is in accordance with good instincts, in no way demoralising, and in every way healthy. Their free action exactly accommodates things to the requirements both of individuals and of the times.

What we are now contemplating is the state of things which will be brought about when the natural action of capital, and the natural action of landed property, have been left to take their own unimpeded course in the valley: for it is to the actual and the possible conditions of Continental Visp-sides, viewed in connection with the actual and the possible conditions of Continental cities, rather than to the broad acres and busy cities of wealthy England, that what I am now saying belongs, notwithstanding the appearance, which is unavoidable, of a constant reference to ourselves. Their case is not quite identical with ours, either in their existing conditions, or their future possibilities, as will be seen in due time and place, when we come to the distinct, and separate, consideration of our own case. Surplus capital, then, and capital withdrawn from business, will always be seeking investment: and as the land of a country is the natural reservoir for a large proportion of all such capital; and as every acre of land is, on our supposition, saleable, as much so as a sack of wheat, or a horse, though at the moment the owner may not be tempted by the price that would be offered for it;

and as much of the land everywhere is always actually in the market, and on sale; the habit of looking to land as the safest both of temporary and of final investments, will become pretty general amongst all classes of people engaged in business. And amongst the holders of land, those who may wish to woo fortune by going into business, and to increase their incomes by investing the price of their land in some good security, will have nothing to withhold them from disposing of it. Estates, that are now in process of formation, will inevitably, when children have to be provided for, or upon the occurrence of any of those other causes we have already referred to, sooner or later enter upon the reverse process of subdivision. The great points to be kept in mind are that every acre, though it may not be actually in the market, is yet, at the will of its owner, marketable; and that, whatever may be the will of its present holder, must, sooner or later, come on the market; and that capital, availing itself of these facilities, naturally takes the direction of the land—in the long run, and to the majority of mankind, the most desirable of all investments; and that this maintains at a high figure the number of proprietors, that class which it is for the interest of the country should be as large as possible: it is obvious that this class will be large, in the era of capital, in every country where the land is within the reach of every man who has capital, exactly in proportion to the amount of capital he is desirous of investing in it.

This state of things appears to have some advantages. These may be summed up in the general remark that it is in complete conformity with the wants and conditions of an era of capital, such as that in which we live. Let us, however, endeavour to resolve this general remark into its constituent elements. As land is the most attractive of human possessions, the one possession which gives a man a place of his own to stand on in this world, it ought naturally to attract to itself much of the surplus capital of the day, and of capital that is being withdrawn from business. In the state of things, we have been just considering, there is no hindrance to the operation of this tendency. This flow of capital towards the land will make it far more productive than it ever has been under any other system. For capital is nothing in the world but bottled-up labour, reconvertible, at the will of the holder, into actual labour, and the implements and materials and products of labour; and this system secures the advantage that the proprietors shall generally be men who have much capital in proportion to their land; and much of this capital will, of course, be applied to it. More land will be reclaimed, more rocks blasted and buried; irrigating canals and cultivation will be carried higher up the sides of the mountains; and more costly means of cultivation applied than are possible under either the peasant-proprietor system, or the large estate system. And this may be a state of things which will not dissatisfy the economist.

It is a state of things which the modern statesman, also, ought to regard with approval; because the possession of land has always, everywhere, been the conservative element in human societies; and the wide diffusion of the proprietorship of land is the only effectual means by which the statesman of the present day can hope to balance, and neutralise, the disturbing action of the large aggregations of population capital has called into being in the great commercial, and manufacturing cities of this era of capital. It ought to be a pleasing, and reassuring sight to him to behold streams of capital and of proprietors constantly flowing off from them towards the land: for in these streams he knows that power is being drawn off from those terrible centres of possible disturbance, which cause him so much anxiety; and that what is thus drawn off from them is being added to the conservative elements of society. So that if the order of society, or any valuable, but, at the moment, misunderstood, institution—misunderstood because things are in an unnatural state—should have to sustain a shock, there would be less power on the side of those who might originate it, and more on the side of those who would have to bear the brunt of it—a state of things which would, probably, prevent the shock from ever occurring. Whereas to array on one side the land of a country held by a handful of proprietors against on the other side numbers and capital, is both to invite the shock, and at the same time to forbid the existence of the natural means for resisting it.

Many great cities are terrible centres of possible disturbance, just because there are artificial barriers which keep asunder the land and its inhabitants on one side, and the cities with their capital and population on the other side. If things were so that streams of those who had had the energy and intelligence requisite for success, and had succeeded, were constantly flowing off from the cities to the land ; and back-currents of those, who were desirous of seeking fortune, flowing into the towns from the country; and this is what ought to be the state of things in an era of capital ; there would be less opposition of interests and sentiments between the town and the country : they would together form more of an homogeneous system. If the town populations could be brought into some kind of connection with the land, they would then, so far, have given hostages, a material guarantee, to social peace, and order.

Neither will they be dissatisfied who are desirous of seeing property so distributed as to favour as much as possible the moral and intellectual condition of the community. Property will everywhere be diffused ; and never being encumbered more than very temporarily, that is never beyond the life of the encumbered holder, for on our supposition it will always pass from hand to hand perfectly unencumbered in every way, its numerous holders in every locality will be in a position to do, and to support, whatever need be done, and supported. Take the instance of the support of religion. It would be mischievous under the previously considered system to disestablish a national Church, because as all the surplus produce of the valley, in the form of a rent of 6,000*l.* a-year, is sent out of the valley, there is nothing left in the hands of the population, such as we imagined it had become, to support religion, except in the humblest, that is in a thoroughly unworthy, form. And here we cannot but think about ourselves; and our doing so will contribute somewhat towards bringing us to a better understanding of this particular point. As things now are in this country the portion of the rent which is retained in every parish for the maintenance of religion is in multitudes of cases the only part of the rent that is retained, and spent, on the spot, among those whose labour produces it. No one will deny that this is in many ways an advantage to them. To instance one advantage, it is often the cause of the existence of needed institutions, as was lately seen most conspicuously in the part the clergy took in the establishment and maintenance of schools, which was an undeniable benefit to their poor neighbours, and to the country, though at the same time something besides and beyond what they were bound to do for the maintenance of the knowledge and of the services of religion. In many places, too, it is the only part of the rent which supports in the locality a man of education and refinement; a social and political advantage which cannot be denied, or overlooked. And this appropriation of a small portion of the rent has largely benefited literature, and to some extent science. It also gives us a large number of families, who far outnumber those supported by the great bulk of the rent of the country, and are in a very favourable position for bestowing on their sons the best attainable education, carefully supervised. To them we owe multitudes of those who are at all times doing the country, at home and abroad, good service. We may, at the present moment, take as instances the Lord Chancellor and the Chancellor of the Exchequer, both of whom were brought up in rural parsonages. Surely it would be a local and a national benefit if more of the rent of the land were somewhat similarly conditioned. And perhaps the greater part of it would be under the system we are now considering. And in addition to this much other property in the form of capital, belonging to such owners of the land, would be brought into each locality, some of which would be sunk in the land, and some retained in securities paying interest and dividends, which would be spent on the spot. Under such a state of things there would be abundance of local means for the voluntary support of all needed institutions, and of religion among the rest; and a national establishment would then cease to be the necessity it is now. At all events, should the national provision for the maintenance of religion, which is incidentally a provision, and as things now are very usefully so, for spending a small part of the rent of each parish, often a very small part indeed, in the parish itself, be cancelled, the aspect of things in many places, and the consequences, would be such as to bring many, who are pretty well satisfied with things as they are without thinking why, to join in the cry for free trade in land.

IV. We have been considering three conditions under which the land of the valley may be held; first, that of a thoroughly carried-out system of peasant proprietorship, which is the natural consummation of things when land is the only means of supporting life, or so nearly the only means that other means disturb its action so little that they need not be considered; and which is the cause of its being divided down to the lowest point at which it is capable of supporting life: we then passed to the opposite extreme, to which the name of landlordism has been given; and we came at last to that which would result, and in places has more or less resulted, from the free interaction of land and capital, in this era of capital. We still have to consider how it has been brought about that, in this era of capital, the free interaction of the two, in this country hardly exists at all; what it is that here hinders its existence; and so gives rise to the two abnormal, but closely connected, phenomena, that land is held only in very large aggregations, and that capital is driven away from the proprietorship of land, except in these large aggregations, to seek imaginary investment at home in never-ending bubble schemes, the manufacture of which is as much a trade as that of calico, or sent abroad to be sunk in impossible Honduras railways, the shares of non-existent Californian mines, and the bonds of hardly more existent states.

This, as it is an unnatural state of things, can have been brought about only by the disturbing action of law. What, then, we have to consider now is, how law has stepped in, and hindered the existence of the state of things which the circumstances of the times demand, and which, therefore, would be their natural and normal condition; and, as it seems, would be fraught with so many and such great advantages to individuals and to the country. The general sense of uneasiness, these questions have given rise to throughout society, indicate that in this matter there is something constitutionally wrong.

When I was in the United States in 1867–1868, I was frequently asked how the people of England could tolerate a system—the questioner always supposed that such a result could only be brought about by law—that gave the land of the country to a handful of the population? I always replied 'that it was a natural consequence of our great wealth. A banker, an Australian, a contractor, a merchant or manufacturer, a coal or iron owner, made his million of money, and as he could live very well on 25,000*l.* a-year, he sunk it in land for the sake of the security the land offered, and because, moreover, its possession gave certain social and political advantages. That it was the competition of these millionaires, who were willing to pay for something beyond the productive powers of the land, that kept small purchasers out of the market, and also induced small holders to sell.' I gave this answer because I wished to avoid a long explanation, involving probably a great deal of argument; and I had not crossed the Atlantic to give, but to receive, information.

I knew at the time that my answer was only a partial one; that it omitted some very important elements of the question; and, therefore, was worth very little, except for the purpose in view at the moment.

For instance; it rested on the assumption that the interest of money is now so high in this country that under no circumstances—I admit that it is so under existing circumstances—would people hold small amounts of land, say a thousand acres, because they could get a better income by selling the land, and investing the proceeds otherwise; and that none can afford to buy land, except those who can afford to buy so much that the moderate interest of the purchase will still in its amount be sufficient for all their wants. It is acknowledged that at present it is so. The whole question, then, turns on the point of what causes it to be so? Is it unavoidable and natural? If so, then it is all right as it is; and the subject is withdrawn from the category of useful discussions.

I, however, for one, am disposed to think that it is neither unavoidable nor natural. There is not such a great difference between the interest of money in France and in England, as to make the great bulk of the people of France desire, above all things, land, and the great bulk of the people of England quite indifferent about it, and even the few who have it in moderate extents desirous of getting rid of it. And, again, in the United States the interest of money is higher than it is here, and yet the ownership of land is regarded as the support, and its cultivation as the natural employment of, I suppose, four-fifths of the whole white population. To us, who look across the Atlantic, the cities appear to be America. But this is an optical illusion. The United States are as large as the whole of Europe, and the cities, though centres of extraordinary activity, are few and far between. Its vast occupied area maintains an agricultural population ; and its agriculture is carried on upon so grand a scale that, when the eye is directed to it, everything else is utterly lost to view. The towns are nothing in a scene which takes in fifteen hundred miles of farm-houses from New York to Omaha, which begin again in the Great Salt Lake Valley, and again on the slopes of the Sierra-Nevada, reaching to the shore of the Pacific.

The cause, then, why what does take place in France, and in the United States, does not take place here, must be sought for in something peculiar to ourselves. And our English peculiarity I believe to be this, that here the dominant and regulative fact bearing on the distribution of land is, that it is not distributable ; in plain English, that it is not saleable. This is brought about by the law which allows estates to be settled, that is to be taken out of the market and practically to be rendered unsaleable. This being the general fact with respect to land, the millions connected with its cultivation, seeing no opening for their ever becoming possessed of an acre of it, do not save for this purpose, and have their thoughts turned in other directions, that is to say, to the towns, to trade, or to emigration. And the rest of the population, being met by the same obstacle, have their thoughts with respect to land, and the investment in it of their capital, equally shaped and coloured by the existence of that obstacle. That which is the dominant fact brings about what is the general feeling and practice. Where is the rural district in which, from the general condition of things, it could become a general practice among the population to work, and deny themselves, in order to acquire some property in the land? Unsaleability is the general rule, and so this motive, and everything that would be connected with it, and grow out of it, has no existence. The same cause acts even in a higher degree on the rest of the population, because their thoughts are not, from the circumstances and character of their lives, so naturally directed towards the land. It would be just the reverse if every acre, everywhere, were always saleable: of course not always on sale, but always saleable at the will of its owner.

Speaking generally, we are in the unique and anomalous position of a nation which has no class of proprietors of small, and moderate-sized estates, cultivating their own land. If circumstances were at all favourable to the maintenance amongst us of such a class, I believe it would be maintained, and would go on increasing. What is the case is, that circumstances adverse to it, and even destructive of it, have been created artificially. By the power of settling estates, large settled estates have everywhere been called into existence. Thenceforth the fight in each neighbourhood is between large settled estates and small properties. The large settled estates are endowed, practically, with perpetuity, and they have within themselves great powers of purchasing, that is of extension; for their owners are already wealthy, and have, also, the power of discounting, for the purpose of making purchases, the future increase in value of their estates; and they always have a strong motive for making such purchases. The small properties, as things now are, have very little of the element of perpetuity; generally no self-contained power of extension by purchase; and their proprietors have no special motives for attempting to extend them. The absorption, then, of the small properties is inevitable; and has been, indeed, almost entirely effected already. Our system creates the large estates, and endows them with the power of swallowing up the small ones; and so year by year takes the land, more and more, out of the market: the general result being that at last we have come to have only a handful of very wealthy rent-receiving proprietors, and few cultivating proprietors; and that the thoughts, the prospects, and the capital of the richest nation in the world are all pretty completely turned away from the land.

We said that our system was not either unavoidable or natural. We ought, therefore, to show how it could have been avoided. We partially did this when we pointed out its causes. Let us, however, endeavour now to find for ourselves a distinct answer to the question, In what way could its growth and establishment have been prevented? I need not repeat its peculiarities: they have just been referred to. Suppose, then, a century ago, the Legislature had come to be of opinion that it was contrary to public policy that an existing generation should have its hands tied, in dealing with the land of the country, by the necessities, or the personal and family ambitions, or the ideas, of preceding generations; and that public policy required that the land of the country should pass from hand to hand perfectly free, each successive holder having an absolute interest in it; receiving, and transmitting it, quite unencumbered, precisely in the same way as a sovereign passes from hand to hand. And that, therefore, it had been enacted, with the view of securing these conditions, that land should not be charged in any way; that it should not be encumbered with any uses, or settlements of any kind; and that there should be no power of mortgaging it beyond the life, or tenancy, of the mortgagor. Such an enactment, it is obvious, would have rendered the existence of the present system impossible. It would have had this effect, because no one having had the power of encumbering land in favour of his widow and younger children, those whose property was only land, would have been obliged to provide for their widows and younger children by bequeathing to them certain portions of the land itself. This would have subdivided the large estates. It, also, would have secured to every owner the power of at any time selling his land, if for any reason he were desirous of so dealing with it. It is, then, presumably, the permission of the very opposite to that which would have prevented the present state of things from existing, that has given it existence.

We have been speaking of what might have been done. Let us look at something that has been done. The course of recent legislation upon this subject is very instructive; and, as far as it goes, is confirmatory of what we have been saying as to both the cause, and the remedy, of existing evils. We often hear remarks made upon the mischievous consequences of land being held in mortmain. But the fact is, that in this country there is no such thing as land held in mortmain. The Legislature has seen the ill effects of its being so held, and, by a series of Acts, all having the same object, has released what was so held. The estates vested in the Ecclesiastical Commission were made saleable in 1843; the episcopal and capitular estates in 1851; the estates of all other ecclesiastical corporations in 1860; of universities and colleges in 1858. The estates of schools and charities, and of municipal bodies, are now in the same state. By this series of enactments the Legislature has, I believe, completely abolished the holding of land in mortmain. It could not, we may be sure, have done otherwise. There was among all enlightened people an overwhelmingly preponderant perception of what ought to be done; and it was comparatively easy to deal with that portion of the land of the country to which these enactments apply. The ground they took was not that the corporate estates had a worse body of tenants, or were worse cultivated than settled estates, for that was not the case, but that it was an evil that land should not be saleable; and so some, that was not saleable before, was made saleable.

And now let us see how these Acts have worked. There have been instances in which incumbents of parishes have sold their glebes, and colleges some of their estates. But who have been the purchasers of these glebes and college estates? As far as I can hear, in every instance the purchasers have been large landed proprietors. And they did no wrong in buying them. Reader, had you and I been in their places we should have done just what they did. The result, however, has been that the large estates have become larger; that is to say, the amount of land that was, through settlements, practically unsaleable, is now greater than it was before; and that through legislation which had for its aim to make land saleable. The present system was so widely established, so powerful, and so ready and so able to avail itself of every opportunity, that there was no possibility of its being otherwise. The fate, then, of that portion of the previously mortmain-held land that has been sold, shows how our existing system works; and enables us to see by an instance, which, though not great in amount, is yet distinct and palpable, the tendency in our large settled estates to continue growing, and by so doing to diminish the amount of saleable land in the country. If, instead of being misled by names, we look at facts, the true mortmain-held land of this country is the settled estates.

The corporate lands are, probably, worth somewhere about 30,000,000*l*. An idea is afloat that there will be a proposal to sell these, and to capitalise the price. But one can hardly suppose that many, except 'adjacent' proprietors, will be found to support the scheme, after people have seen what has become of such portions of these lands as have already been sold under the recent Acts just referred to; and when they remember that the discharge of certain duties is attached to the revenues of these corporate and endowment estates. And if these duties are not always discharged satisfactorily, that is a matter which better superintendence might set right. At all events, it is better for the public that they should get out of these estates something, than that they should get nothing. If the public desire that it should be so, the Legislature, we may be sure, will be ready enough to see that all endowments are turned to good account.

We frequently hear the remark, and it is made as if it explained the existence and the character of our present system, that feudalism still flourishes in this country. This is very wide indeed of the mark. There are many, we may be sure, who would be disposed to think that it would be of advantage if something like the division of land of the feudal times still obtained amongst us. The records of the Exchequer give the number of knights' fees at 60,215. Let that, however, be as it may, our system is as unlike that of feudalism as anything can be. It belongs in its whole character to the era of capital, but in the form a land-system must assume; and this is its distinguishing feature, when the flow of capital to the land has been so interfered with as practically to prohibit its investment in land, except by very rich people, in very large amounts; that is to say, by people who already have a great deal of land, or who have a great deal of capital. This is an artificial state of things belonging to the era of capital. The natural state of things in the era of capital would be the direct opposite: for that would issue in there being a multitude of owners of estates, purchased and used for all manner of purposes; and to all the land being marketable; and, indeed, to a considerable portion of it, everywhere, being at any time in the market.

Both of these states, the artificial and the natural one, are equally possible in the era of capital. The first is brought about, when, as I have pointed out, the action of the law favours perpetuity, unsaleability, and agglomeration. The latter, when all the land is saleable; and everyone who has capital, no matter whether much or little, is able to buy. There is no feudalism in either of these two states of things. The former is a factitious kind of capitalism.

It may sound paradoxical, after what has been said, to announce that the change suggested in our present system would have the effect of raising the price of land: I am, however, of opinion that it would have this paradoxical effect; because, though it would largely increase the supply, it would in a still greater degree increase the demand for, and the uses of land. It would make all who have capital possible purchasers, and would be an inducement to many, particularly among those whose work is on the land, to save capital in order that they might become purchasers. It would bring into play and activity a great variety of motives for purchasing. For instance; we should then see joint-stock companies buying land which offers no particular advantages for residence, for the single purpose of manufacturing food out of it. They would pour capital into it in such amounts as only proprietors, who were also joint-stock companies, could. They would drain, mix soils, employ steam machinery for cultivation, for preparing artificial manures, and for cutting, crushing, and cooking food for cattle; they would build beet-sugar factories, or whatever else would pay when done well, and on a large scale. Other districts adapted to small properties, if such there be, we should see falling into the hands of small proprietors. Others again, which from their salubrity, or beauty, or local proximity to large towns, were adapted for residential purposes, we should see turned to this account: so that in places where now there may be one, or perhaps not one, resident proprietor, there would be a hundred, or a thousand. In these days of railways and capital all this is natural: and as it is natural it is what would be best for us. I cannot see anything bad in such a state of things; and I think it is what will be brought about eventually. If it had existed during the last fifty years, probably a large portion of the 1,000,000,000*l.* of capital that have been sent out of the country, would have been kept at home. If there were perfect freedom in dealing with the land, in this rich and populous country, the price of agricultural land would rise to a higher price than it has attained in Switzerland, Belgium, and parts of France, where it has long been selling for more than it sells for here. If a joint-stock company were to demonstrate that 25*l.* of capital per acre applied to the cultivation of 1,000 acres was a profitable speculation, would that have any tendency to lower the value of land?

I believe that some of us will live to see the joint-stock principle introduced into farming, or rather applied to the ownership and cultivation of the land. My reason for believing this is, that it has been found to answer in everything else; and that I can see no other way in which capital, to the amount required in these days, can be applied to the land; and that I can see in the nature of the case no reason why it should not be so applied to the land. I take it for granted that, at this moment, land can be cultivated more productively, and more economically, comparing the amount of produce with the cost of producing it, in farms of about 1,000 acres each, cultivated highly, and by steam machinery, than in any other fashion. If it be so, then the system must force its way to general adoption; and to the looker-on, practically, no question remains uncertain but that of time. If he is satisfied that it is the natural system in the era of capital, he knows that, sooner or later, it must come. One of its pre-requisites, which it will take time to bring about, is, that the land should be owned by those who cultivate it; probably, in each case, by a firm. Whether the firm consist of three or four partners, or of three or four dozen shareholders, will make no difference. On no other conditions will the costly plant be provided, or the inducement in the way of profits be sufficient.

The past history of agriculture will here help us in our attempt to understand its future. The aboriginal agricultural implement was, as we all know, a burnt stick — a broken branch, with its point hardened in the fire. That was in the stone era, and so the forest could not be felled. Only here and there a small plot could be cultivated with such an implement. The rest of the land, that is to say almost the whole of it, was a game preserve for wild animals, deer, wild cattle, wild hogs, &c. After nobody knows how many ages of this style of farming, and of utilising the land, came the discovery of metals. An iron hoe was then regarded as a more wonderful machine than a steam-plough is now. It was beyond the means of any individual, except perhaps here and there a great chief. Villages may have clubbed together the few articles they had of exchangeable value, that is to say became a joint-stock company, to secure the possession of one of these marvellous implements. Whatever the land had yielded to the tillage of the burnt stick, and through the game preserves, it now yielded a great deal more. The game preserves still continued: but with respect to animal food also there had been a little advance, for domestic animals now began to appear in the village. One advance always draws on others. But the domestic animals were at first kept only in small numbers, for they wandered over large expanses of land, almost exclusively forest; the game still remaining the more important of the two. This was the second stage. But as time goes on iron, and the domestic animals, become more abundant; and an ox, or so many ox-hides, can be exchanged for a hoe. It is now possible to get so much more food out of the land, that one man can raise enough for the support of two. This immediately leads to slavery, which always makes its appearance in rude societies as soon as they have reached the point at which one man can produce more food than is sufficient for himself. This advances agriculture some steps further. Cattle become abundant; labour is abundant; and a sufficiency of iron is procurable. The forest is, therefore, taken in hand, and fields, that is spaces where the trees have been felled, are formed. And now the plough appears on the scene, and civilised society is fairly under weigh. Cultivation continues to extend, and with cultivation pasturage. The forest gradually disappears, and domestic animals entirely take the place of wild game, except for purposes of amusement and luxury. And so on up to the system with which we are all familiar. Every discovery advanced matters a step, and made the land more productive. As, for instance, the introduction of artificial grasses and roots, for our ancestors in the autumn used to kill and salt the beef and mutton they would require for the winter and spring. Then came a better supply of manures, and the two together rendered the abandonment of fallows possible. The land has all along been a constant quantity. It, from the beginning, has been the same. But its produce has from the first been increasing through never-ceasing advances in the means and methods of cultivating it and of turning it to account.

And now another advance is in sight, that of cultivation by steam. This implies a great deal. In each stage there grew out of the nature of things, as they then were, a certain definite proportion between the means used and the amount of land cultivated as one concern. In the burnt stick era the little cultivated plots might have shown in the forest as the stars do in the field of heaven. In the hoe-period they were multiplied and enlarged as the stars appear to us through a telescope. Then we had peasant proprietors, and small tenants. The number and size of the luminous, that is, of the cultivated, plots were increasing, as means and appliances increased and improved. And now we suppose that a farm ought properly to be of 400 or 500 acres in extent. This means that the instruments of production and our organisation have advanced very greatly. So must it be with steam cultivation : each concern must be on a large scale. I have supposed that not less than 1,000 acres will be necessary for turning to good account the machinery that will be required for tilling the soil, and gathering in the crops, and preparing them for market, for preparing food for the stock, and for making artificial manures, &c. No existing buildings will be of any use. Everything will have to be constructed for the purposes required. Land, therefore, that has to be cultivated in this way must be regarded as quite unprovided with the necessary plant, as much so as a thousand acres of the prairie of Colorado, or of the Pampas of La Plata. And as nobody will invest all this costly fixed plant on other people's land, the land must be owned by those who are to cultivate it in this way. But the purchasing, the providing with such plant, and the so cultivating a thousand acres will require not less than 75,000*l.* This, at present at all events, is quite beyond a farmer's means. It can, therefore, speaking generally, only be done by firms or companies. If it will pay, they will do it. Lord Derby tells us the land ought to yield twice as much as it does now. We may, I suppose, set the present gross produce of good average land fairly farmed at 10*l.* an acre. If land highly cultivated by steam, and with the liberal application of capital we are supposing, would advance its produce to only half of Lord Derby's supposed possible increase, the gross yield would be 15*l.* an acre. And this might give, after allowing one-third for working expenses, deterioration, and insurance, 13¾*l.* per cent. on the investment ; but we will put the working at half, which will leave a profit of 10 per cent. If this could be done, then the streams of English capital that are perennially flowing off into all countries would be profitably diverted to the cultivation and enrichment of our own land; and no small portion of the other millions we are year by year paying the foreigner for food, might be paid to food-manufacturers of our own, and so saved to the country.

France produces at home its own sugar; and, besides, sends to us 60,000 tons a-year. We do not manufacture sugar at home, because an English tenant would not spend 8,000*l*., if he had it, in erecting a sugar factory on another man's land; but such firms of proprietors could, and probably would, on their own.

Capital swept away the peasant proprietor. It has almost swept away the 50-acre tenant. And it will sweep away the 250-acre tenant. But it offers to all better careers than those it closes against them. The system it is bringing upon us will employ more hands, and will require them all to be better men, and will pay them all better, both for their work and for their capital. Under it there will be openings everywhere for everyone to become what he is fit to become. This will be a premium on education; and it will do more to suppress drunkenness in the rural districts than any conceivable licensing, or permissive, or prohibitory Acts.

I do not know what, under such a state of things, will become of our old friend, who was also the friend of our forefathers—the agricultural pauper. On a farm of a thousand acres, carried on in the fashion we have been supposing, there would be no place for him. Upon its area there would not be a man who was not wanted. And all who were wanted would be well paid and well housed. There would be engine-men, and stock tenders, and horsemen, and labourers, more in number perhaps than the hands now employed on the same space, but all would be better off, and would be better men. In order, however, that this may be brought about, capital must be allowed free access to the land, that is to say, the land must be set free.

The argument from the picturesque will not arrest the course of events. Never was the country so picturesque as when there was no cultivation at all, and the noble savage pursued his wild game through the primæval forest over hill and dale. The little hoed plots of a succeeding epoch were a great encroachment on the picturesque. The fields that came in with the plough carried the disfigurement still further. Our hedges and copses, under the existing system, are rapidly disappearing. But the human interest in the scene has always been increasing: and it will culminate when the steam-engine shall have brought in a system under which those who do the very lowest forms of labour then required will be better fed, and housed, and clothed, and paid, because it will be a system that will not admit of bad work, than was possible under previous systems, which did not depend for their success on the intelligence of the labourer, and the accuracy and excellence of his work.

Such a system would carry out to their logical and ultimate consummation the free interaction of capital and agricultural land. All such land, the implements, and whole plant employed in its cultivation, and even the labour, skill, and intelligence of its cultivators, would be represented by dividend-receiving, 10*l.*, 5*l.*, or 1*l.* share certificates, transferable merely by the double endorsement of the seller and of the buyer. The old certificate, thus endorsed, would be presented to the manager, if necessary by post; and a new certificate would be issued to the new holder. These certificates would circulate almost as freely as money; but as it would be a kind of money that would carry a dividend at the rate of capital employed in safe ventures, say four-and-a-half or five per cent., with a prospect of improvement, wherein it would differ from the low interest of Exchequer bills, the holding of such certificates would be the most attractive kind of savings' bank to the poor, and to all. The great difficulty in the way of saving in the case of the poor, and of all who are unacquainted with business, is to find suitable, and safe, investments. That difficulty would be removed; and they would be enabled to participate, according to their means, as easily, and on the same footing, as the richest and the best informed, in the wealth and property of the country. Any labourer on any joint-stock farm, or elsewhere, any artisan, any servant girl, any poor governess, who might save a few pounds, might invest them in a share or two; and the increment, whether earned or unearned, in the value of land, and of its produce, would go to them proportionally with the wealthiest. Everyone would, in this way, have opened to him an avenue for participating, to any amount possible to him, in the possession of the land everywhere. A large proportion of the population would thus become interested in the development of its resources, and so in the prosperity of the country, and in the order and stability of society. The land would, in a sense, become mobilised; and the possession of it rendered capable of universal diffusion. Any one of the present owners, who might come to wish that any portion of his land might be held, and used, in this fashion, might receive, if he chose to be so paid, as many shares in each concern formed out of it, as would equal the value of land he might make over to it.

If the possibility of such a system could be demonstrated, the existing owners of land might be the first to wish to see it carried out. The following figures will show why. Suppose a thousand acres of agricultural land is letting at what is about the average rent of such land, that is at about 30*s*. an acre, the landlord will be receiving for it 1,500*l*. a year, subject to some not inconsiderable deductions. But if this same land were sold to a cultivating firm at 50*l*. an acre, the price being received in shares, and the concern were to pay to original shareholders 10 per cent. the rent of 1,500*l*., subject to deductions, would have become a dividend of 5,000*l*. subject to no deductions. But we will suppose only 3,000*l*., for that will be double the present rent, and so quite sufficient for our argument.

So far as the system might be adopted would ownership of the land of the old kind cease, and in its place be substituted, in convenient amounts, dividend-receiving, easily transferable, and freely circulating capital stock certificates, within everybody's reach, secured upon definite portions of the agricultural land of the country, representing its present value, and participating in its future advances in value. Such certificates would, also, offer an improving security for trust funds of all kinds, and for endowments.

The combination of what I have observed, during a life in the country, of the requirements of land, and of the condition and wants of the poor, with my experience of the duties of a trustee (which have devolved upon me to, perhaps, an unusually great extent), suggested to me the ideas I have just been endeavouring to present to the reader. If they are practicable they may contribute to the solution of existing difficulties of several kinds. I am aware that they cannot do this, because in that case they would be quite visionary, if they are not in harmony with the natural requirements and conditions of the era of capital. That they would have been impracticable in other times does not prove that they would be impracticable now.

But we have been enticed off the main line of our discussion to a by-path, which was offering a very interesting view into the future. We must now return to the point we had before reached, which was that of the popular misconceptions that are held with respect to our existing system. There are, then, again, others who suppose that its salient peculiarities may be explained by a reference to what is frequently spoken of as 'The Law of Primogeniture.' We have, however, in this country no law of primogeniture in any sense that can be intended in such a reference. There is no body of rights attaching by law to the eldest son. The extent of what may be regarded as law in this matter is the right of the eldest son of a peer to succeed to his father's peerage; and of the eldest sons of those who have hereditary titles to succeed to their father's titles. The power of entailing landed property only acts in favour of the system of primogeniture, because the holders of landed property themselves choose to work it in this direction; for it might be used equally in favour of equal partition. There is then no law of primogeniture in the sense supposed. A man who buys land, or in any way comes to have the absolute disposal of it, as the word absolute implies, may dispose of it as he pleases. He may, if such should be his wish, leave it all to his youngest child, or in equal partition amongst all his children. Only, should he die intestate, the law will deal with his land (but we have just been told that this is to be altered) in the way in which, looking at the conduct in this matter of English landlords generally, it may be supposed the man himself would have dealt with it had he made a will. Possibly he may not have made a will because he knew that the law would so dispose of it. The law in the few exceptional cases of this kind that arise from time to time, recognises, and acts on, the state of opinion and sentiment which has grown out of the power, it had itself given, of charging and encumbering land —a power which probably had no very glaring economical evils and inconveniences in an age when the population of the country was only a third of what it is at present, and when capital was only in an embryonic condition, and when, too, perhaps the political system this power upheld appeared to be necessary.

It is not, then, any law of primogeniture which has brought about our present land system, but certain powers, conferred by law, which have suggested to people the desirability of acting on, and enabled them to act on, the voluntarily adopted principle of primogeniture; that is to say the power of charging and encumbering their estates. And, now that the era of capital is upon us, it is not improbable that the policy of continuing this power will be debated, for at such a time it has some very obvious evils and inconveniences. I do not mean that it will be reconsidered by the legislature before many years have elapsed, or in the first instance; for in a matter of this kind the legislature can do nothing but give form and sanction to what the circumstances of the times have already settled. If it shall be generally felt that the ill consequences of the exercise of this power overbalance its advantages, we may suppose that it will be withdrawn. This is not a question that will be much affected by any amount of speaking or writing, if that be all. If the facts of the matter are of themselves not felt as evils and inconveniences, no amount of speaking or of writing will bring people so to regard them. But should they come to be so felt, the people of this country will be desirous of dealing with them as all men, always and everywhere, have dealt with such matters, when they were seen to admit of removal. But however that may be, it is not a law of primogeniture, but certain law-conferred powers, enabling people to act on the principle of primogeniture, which are the cause of the existing state of things in this matter.

In the discussion of this subject, which ramifies in many directions, for it has moral and social, as well as economical, political, and constitutional bearings, many questions will be propounded, and will have to be considered: such, for instance, as whether, in these several respects, a comparatively small number of large land-owners is better, in this era of capital, and of large cities, than a large number of land-owners, holding estates varying in dimensions, according to the amounts of capital people would, from a variety of motives, be desirous of investing in land, were all the land of the country free and marketable; or, in other words, whether, in such times, the artificial condition of things we have been considering is safer than, and preferable to, the natural condition? The share-certificates, I just now spoke about, would make it free and marketable to the greatest imaginable degree.

It will also be asked whether it is fair to the land-owner, and, all things considered, advantageous to the community, that he should be obliged to provide for his widow and younger children either by saving the means for making such provision from his income, or by leaving to them, absolutely, what portions of his landed property he may think fit? Those same share-certificates would supply an easy, inexpensive, and safe method of providing for widows and younger children.

Another question will be whether in this era of capital, which means that there will always be some large capitalists as well as many small ones, the liberation of the land would really lead to the extinction of large estates? Largeness is a word of comparative signification. Of course there would be few such large estates as there are now, because that is the result of growth through many generations under the very peculiar circumstances we have been referring to: but if the interchange of land and capital were perfectly free there would be everywhere many considerable estates, though the general order of things might be estates of moderate size, descending to holdings of small extent, which might be the most numerous of all; or such holdings might not be very numerous: for in matters of this kind there is always much that is unforeseen. One point, however, may, I think, be held to be certain: we shall never, in this country, see anything approximating to peasant proprietorship. That is simply inconceivable in the era of capital. Both the land and the man can be turned, now, to better account. Its advocates are either ignorant demagogues, or members of that harmless class who, having their eyes in the back of their heads, can only see, and wish for, what has passed away. If we ever come to have share-estates, such as I have endeavoured to describe, they will, probably, average, as I said, about 1,000 acres each.

It will, perhaps, also, be suggested that there may be some mixed method of proceeding, which, while respecting existing arrangements, would, at the same time, largely increase the number of proprietors ; as, for instance, to deal with the rents of endowments compulsorily, and with those of the owners of land at their option, just as the tithe was dealt with; that is to say, to convert the rent into a permanent charge upon the land ; and then to sell the land, subject to this rent-charge, the yearly value of which would be ascertained, as is done in the case of the tithe commutation rent-charge, by reference to certain averages of the price of the different kinds of grain cultivated in this country. The immediate gain to corporations, and trustees, and to proprietors who might be disposed to sell, would be considerable, for they would continue to get their present rents, without deductions, and would, besides, be able to sell the proprietary right in the land, and its capacity for future increase in value, for whatever they would fetch in the market. This would suit the share-system, for the land might then be bought with or without the rent, as it might happen in each case.

Our opinions on any question are very much in

fluenced by our observation of the direction things are taking. Now, with respect to our existing land-system, all changes in matters connected with, or bearing upon, it, and which appear to be either imminent, or possible, are likely to take only the direction of what will be unfavourable to its maintenance. For instance, if it be decided that endowments, now consisting of land, should be capitalised, in order that more land may be brought into the market, the line of argument, that triumphed against them, will be equally available against our existing land-system. And, furthermore, if the lands belonging to charities, institutions, and corporations be sold, it is evident that, as things now are, they will, for the most part, be bought up by the owners of large contiguous estates; so that, in fact, the remedy attempted will only make the evil it was intended to remedy, more glaring: the great estates will have become greater. The fate of the corporate estates, thus compulsorily sold, will be that of the thousands of small properties the large estates have of late years swallowed up. Everybody knows that many houses of the gentry of former times are now farm-houses on every large estate. It cannot be otherwise, for this is how a large estate is formed. All the smaller estates in the neighbourhood, just like the meteoric bodies which come at last to be overpowered by the attraction of our planet, must, as things are now, gravitate towards it: their end is, sooner or later, generally the former, to fall into it. So, if the estates of the endowments are sold, will it be with them. It has been so with those that have been already sold.

Again, if the Church be disestablished and disendowed, a certain proportion of the rent of each parish in the country, pretty generally more or less increased by private income, will cease to be spent within the parish. What is so spent at present, as far as it goes, and to a great extent in many cases, lessens the hard and repellent features of the absenteeism of the owners of the land in those parishes. Disendowment, therefore, will make the evils and inconveniences of the present system, whatever they may be, more felt, and more conspicuous; and a better mark, as they will then stand clear of all shelter, for adverse comment.

So, too, if the agricultural land of this country should continue, and there is no reason for supposing the contrary, to fall, year by year, into fewer hands, the strength of those who will have to defend the system will be diminishing at the very time that wealth, intelligence, numbers, union, and every element of power, are increasing on the side of those who cannot see that they have any interest in maintaining it.

If the recent Education Act have the intended effect of educating the millions who have no landed property, the most coveted of all human possessions, will they find anything in the existing system that

H

will commend it to their favour? Will they not rather be in favour of a system, which would make every acre of land in the country marketable?

If people should come to think that the reason why France, notwithstanding the abject condition of a large proportion of its peasant-proprietors, and without our stupendous prosperity in manufactures and commerce, has become so rich, is that it keeps its savings at home, because the land of the country is marketable, while we, every year, scatter tens of millions of pounds of our savings all over the earth to be utterly lost, because they cannot be invested at home in the land of the country, the natural reservoir, or savings' bank, of the surplus capital of a country, as well as the best field for its employment, will they not go on to wish that the land here, too, could be made marketable?

If population and capital go on increasing, may we not anticipate that this will engender a desire—for in these days of railways and telegraphs it is much the same where a man lives—that the agricultural land of the country should be brought into the state of divisibility and marketableness, into which some of the land in the neighbourhood of our great cities has been brought through the pressure of circumstances? This pressure may extend, and be felt with respect to the land of the whole country.

In an era, too, when popular principles so thoroughly pervade society as to influence all our legislation, is it probable that a system which is the reverse of popular will commend itself to general acceptance? It is also on the cards now that manual labour may become so costly as to necessitate, if a great deal of land is not to go out of cultivation, the substitution of machinery to such an extent as will be done, generally, only by those who own the land.

The whole stream of tendency, then, both in what is now occurring, and in what is likely to occur in no remote future, seems setting strongly in a direction which cannot be regarded as favourable to the maintenance of our present land-system. And the observation of this will, sooner or later, consciously or unconsciously, very much modify opinion on the subject; for in human affairs, just as with respect to the operations of Nature, we are disposed to acquiesce in what we have come to understand is inevitable.

But we have for some time lost sight of the Valley of the Visp, though not of its imaginary sole Proprietor. He has all along been before us. What we have been considering was how, in this era of capital, he came to be its sole proprietor, what are the action and effects of those artificial conditions which placed him in this position, and what are the chances of the maintenance of these artificial conditions.

Things move fast in these days: but few people expect that any change will take place in his time. He will continue in the position of social eminence, and of political power, he now occupies. He will go on hoping to leave after him a line of descendants occupying the same, or even a greater, position. This will be the dominant motive in his mind. If any land is to be bought in his neighbourhood, there will still be a likelihood that he will become the purchaser of it. It has always been so, since the estate became the predominant one in those parts. And that it should be so is now regarded almost as a law of nature; as something quite inevitable; so that no one need enquire whether it is beneficent in its action, or otherwise. If he have not cash in hand to pay for the new purchase, he will mortgage his property to the amount of the price. In this era of capital the value of land goes on increasing, and so the mortgage will in time be paid off by the estate itself. In this way, in these times, every large estate has within itself, even without Austrian marriages,[1] a progress-generated power of absorption and growth. Without lessening the area of the estate, he will provide for those who are dependent on him by charging it with the payment of whatever he may please to leave them: so that while no very apparent injustice will be done to them, the position of the single representative of the family will not be affected, for he will still appear before the world as the owner of the whole estate. He will also hope that, from time to time, the representatives of the family will, by making pur-

---

[1] Bella gerant alii. Tu felix Austria nube:
Nam, quæ Mars aliis, dat tibi regna Venus.

chases in the way in which he has, and by the introduction of great heiresses into the family, increase the extent of the estate.

At times, when he hears how demagogues are raving about the nationalisation of the land, and the tyranny of capital; and when he visits the valley, and sees the condition of many, indeed of all the people on the estate, he may feel that he is in a somewhat invidious position. But he will feel also that no one is to blame: his progenitors could not well have acted otherwise than as they did; nor could he well act otherwise than as he is acting, and will act. And those who are discussing the matter, sometimes with the tone of men who are suffering a wrong, would, we may be sure, not act otherwise, under the circumstances, themselves.

Suppose, however, that for the restricted and artificial action of capital, which has brought this state of things about, its natural action has been substituted: what will be the effect on the hopes, and on the family, of the proprietor of our valley? We may venture to predict that the natural order of things will give him a securer chance of realising his hopes in their best sense. His family will start, in the race of life, in possession of the whole of the land of the valley. For them this will be no bad start. The land of the valley will bear division for several generations without reducing the members of the family to a bad position, even if none of them should do anything at all to improve their position. But this, judging by the ordinary principles of human nature, we may be sure, speaking generally, will not be the case. Two centuries hence, it will be their own fault, if, instead of the family being really only one man, they have not become a clan in the valley: a clan possessed of more social importance, and of more political influence, than could attach to a family represented by a single member. Some will have become invigorated by the inducements to exertion that will have come home to them, and by the wholesome consciousness in each that he is somewhat dependent on himself for maintaining and improving his position. Whatever efforts to advance themselves they may come to make, will not be made under unfavourable circumstances. None of them will have occasion to feel, as perhaps some of their ancestors at times had, that they are in an invidious position; and none will regard them with feelings that, if not 'somewhat leavened with a sense of injustice,' do yet arise from a suspicion that things are not quite as they ought to be, through there having been some kind of interference with their natural course. Is not this a nobler, a more patriotic, a more human, and in every way a better prospect than that which is now feeding the somewhat misdirected paternal ambition of the present proprietor? Would it not be a better anticipation of the fortunes of his family, to think of them as a numerous body of proprietors, occupying a good position, through the natural action of the circumstances and conditions of the times, than to look forward to the uncertain character and uncertain position of a single member of his family, who will be maintained, if maintained, by conditions, on the permanency of which no dependence can be placed, because they are at discord with the needs and circumstances of the times?

Land now no longer rules. Capital is king. Capital it is that does everything now; that even, but under abnormal and artificial conditions, aggregates our large estates. Under this dynasty the advantages the land is capable of conferring on man are not withdrawn, but much increased both in degree and in variety; and everything desirable, the land not excepted, becomes, in a manner and degree inconceivable in all foregone times, the reward of personal exertion and worth. This is what distinguishes this dynasty from those that have preceded it. If it be the true king, it will prove its legitimacy, by removing all artificial barriers to the development and exercise of its beneficent powers. If it cannot do this, it is a bastard dynasty, and will be dethroned.

V. But I have not yet exhausted all the possible forms in which land may be held. Their name is legion. Every country, and every condition of society, has had, has now, and will have, its own. I say nothing of the serf-system: that among civilised nations has gone for ever. So has the system of village communities. The co-operative system, however, has believers, and, it appears possible, may have a trial. But I, for one, because I believe in capital, and in the individual, have no belief in this kind of co-operation, as a general system, either in manufactures and commerce, or, and that least of all, in agriculture: and, with respect to the latter, whether the co-operators be renters, or owners. Ownership would make no difference at all beyond the power owners would possess of mortgaging their land; and this, as it is a resource that would very soon be exhausted, need not be considered here. The only practical difference would be, that co-operative renters would require a larger extent of land to live from than co-operative owners, whose land was unmortgaged. If the system of co-operation were general, competition, and the increase of population that would have to be provided for, and which would lead either to subdivision, or to an increase of co-operators upon each farm, would inevitably bring the style of living down to a point at which it would be no better than it is now in the Visp Valley. And this is so low a condition of life, both materially and intellectually, that most people are of opinion that it is not worth while to go in for its maintenance, or even, perhaps, to regret its disappearance.

A population of co-operators sunk to this depth, and they could not but sink to it, would, like the old Irish potatovors, or the French petty proprietors, be in a state of chronic wretchedness and degradation: this, in bad seasons, amounts to a state of starvation. If the individual Irish potatovor could not, and the individual French petty proprietor, in whom the parsimonious disposition of his race is exaggerated, rarely can, save, because bad seasons oblige him to mortgage his little plot of land, from which he can hardly extract a living in good seasons, we may be sure that neither would, nor could, such co-operators. I am disposed to prefer the present condition of our agricultural labourers, the most feeble class amongst us. At all events, they have more than one buffer between themselves and bad seasons. First there is the reservoir of capital possessed by the farmer. This is, to the extent of wages, generally, sufficient. In consequence of its existence bad seasons make little or no difference to hired labourers. But under the co-operative system there would be no farmers, but only co-operators, just able to get along in ordinary seasons. Our labourers have, also, a second buffer, which is often of some use to them, in their wealthy neighbours. But under the co-operative system there would probably be no wealthy neighbours. They possess, too, a third buffer in the State, which comes in, in the last resort, to rescue them from the extreme consequences of every kind of calamity. But under a system of peasant co-operators there could hardly be anything resembling our poor-law; for the rationale of that is, that the people who cultivate the soil of the country, are themselves devoid of all property. These three buffers, then, would all have disappeared; and nothing, as far as we can see, would arise, or could be created, to take their place. Such co-operators would be only co-operative peasant-proprietors: which is an absurdity.

Another sufficient objection to this system is, that this is the era of capital, and that such a system would most effectually prohibit the outflow of capital to the land. Capital could no more be invested in the ownings of a wretched population of co-operators, than it could be in the plots of Irish potatovors, or of French petty proprietors.

The conclusion, then, to which my moralising on the spectacle of the Valley of the Visp brought me was, that it belongs to a state of things, which, even in such secluded retreats, will not be able to linger on much longer: at all events, that it is not desirable that it should. We live under the dominion of capital, that is to say, of property other than land, or rather, perhaps, of an accumulated, and still accumulating, interest or dividend-bearing essence of all property (which is labour stored up in some material), reconvertible at will, for productive purposes, into land, labour, or anything men have of exchangeable value. This mighty essence of all property is within the reach of us all, in proportion to our respective opportunities and abilities, and the efforts to gain possession of it we choose to make. But though within the reach of all, it is the mightiest of all magicians; and it is evident that it must modify both the possession, the distribution, and the use of land, as well as everything else with which we have to do. In this there is nothing to be regretted. On the contrary, we ought all of us to congratulate ourselves on the advent of such an era: for it means that our resources for living, and for living well, in respect of all the requirements of human happiness, have been thereby vastly enlarged, and with a power of indefinite enlargement, irrespective of the area of the country. It means, too, that careers have been thereby opened to all, in ways which would have been inconceivable when land supplied the only resource for living; for that now every moral and intellectual endowment, every form of labour, and every aptitude can be turned to account. Even land can be made productive of greater benefits to us than we were wont to derive from it, for capital is showing that it has economical, and other, capacities for improving man's estate, undreamt of by its old cultivators.

Popular language, which is the expression of

popular ideas, on this subject is adequate. It gives correctly the philosophy of the matter. What is wanted is that it should be clearly and generally understood, and used with accuracy. Money has both an intrinsic value as the representative of so much labour expended in the acquisition of the precious metals, and a conventional use as a metallic certificate, entitling its holder to exchange it against anything else in the world anyone has to part with, that costs in its production an equal amount of labour, there being at the time no abnormal disturbance of the ratio of supply and demand. In the latter respect it matters not whether the certificate is on gold or paper : for the paper represents gold, or equal value. When earned, or otherwise acquired, by a kitchen-maid, a speculator, or a prime minister, it may be used in any one of three ways. First, it may be spent. Secondly, it may be hoarded. Thirdly, it may be used as capital. By spending is meant using money for the acquisition of what perishes in the use ; when it passes into another man's hands who again has the option of using it in any one of the three ways. It is evident that a man may spend money for clothing, food, and other necessary purposes, in order to live, and to enable him to do his work in life well, whatever it may be : it is then spent well, and in a sense productively. Or he may spend it on vice, or ostentation, or hurtful pleasures : it is then spent ill. By hoarding is meant putting it away unproductively for future use. This was originally the only alternative to spending. The money stored away in the treasuries of the old Pharaohs was an instance of this unproductive suspension of use. This is still the practice, everywhere, among rude and ignorant people: it is the hybernation of money; its active uses are put in abeyance. As capital it may be used in two ways. It may either be invested, or employed. Investing it means placing it in securities that do not require management, as, for instance, consols, mortgages, the rent of land, &c.; the correlative of which is interest. Employing it means placing it in reproductive industries, as, for instance, in agriculture, manufactures, trade, commerce, &c., which require management, and the correlative of which is profit. This when divided among shareholders, who manage the concern jointly, or by a selection from their body, becomes dividend. This is the highest form of economical organisation. It gives to all, in their respective proportions, however small those proportions may be, the power of employing capital; and to all who have the ability and integrity, the chance of rising to its management. It is the full development of the era of capital. It is the stage we have now reached. It enables the kitchen-maid, and everybody, to participate in the highest advantages of capital. I think we shall see it employed in this way in the cultivation and proprietorship of the land. If so, then, I think the poor and ignorant will have brought home to them a very strong motive for saving, because they will have constantly before their eyes a safe and profitable means of employing their savings. They, too, may thus become capitalists of the best kind.

Two pregnant errors, however, there appear to be, which it will be necessary for us to avoid, especially, in order that, as respects the land, we may secure the natural conditions and natural advantages of our era of capital. One is the error of making people's wills for them directly, in the way done in France. This breaks up the land of a country into properties smaller than they would become under the natural circumstances of the times: thus condemning, through legislation, a large part of the population, deluded by the fallacious disguise of proprietorship, to life-long misery. The other error is that of making people's wills for them indirectly, in the way done in some other countries. This has the opposite effect of agglomerating the land of the country into estates larger than they would become under the natural circumstances of the times, and of reducing the number of proprietors of agricultural land almost to the vanishing point. The first method both increases the number of wretched, degraded, and almost useless proprietors, and diminishes the size of the properties, to a highly mischievous degree. The latter just in proportion as it increases the size of the estates diminishes the number of proprietors. Both limit the variety of uses to which the land may be put. Both introduce causes of political action at variance with the natural conditions of the times. Every system has some advantages: but whatever may be the advantages of the latter, it is, at all events, an interference with the natural rights of each generation, and with the natural course of things; for it prevents the ownership, and the uses, of the land of the country adjusting themselves to the circumstances and the requirements of the times; and hinders the application, to its culture, of that combination of knowledge, energy, and capital, which is manifestly within reach, and has become requisite for developing its productiveness to the degree acknowledged to be possible now, but which cannot be secured under our present landlord-and-tenant system. If, however, this be a serious evil, it is, for reasons already given, one of that class of evils which engender their own remedy.

Many are of opinion that landlordism was all along at the bottom of the evils of Ireland. Landlordism is probably the cause of the Liberalism of Scotch constituencies. If so, what is there to prevent the same cause having, eventually, somewhat similar effects in England? And, if so, then, what next? If, however, the law, instead of interfering with the natural course of things, by indirectly making people's wills for them, would take care that the land of the country should pass from generation to generation, and from hand to hand, free from every kind of encumbrance, and so be all, at all times, at the will of the holder, marketable, a question, which is now causing much anxiety, because it may, before long, give much trouble, would probably die away, and be no more heard of; nor, probably, should we hear any more of the antagonisms, with which we are all now so familiar, between the town and the country. One step, at least, would have been taken towards making us one people.

The stimulus new scenes apply to the mind, more particularly when its owner is passing through them on foot, and alone, accounts for the foregoing chapter. But its having been thought out under such circumstances by A is no reason for its being read by B, who is neither on foot, nor, probably, alone; and the only scene before whom is, doubtless, the not unfamiliar one of his own fireside; one which, perhaps, has never invited, and may, too, be quite unfitted for, either the debate, or the rumination, of such discussions. Still, as it was suggested by, and constructed in the mind during, the tramp I am recording, and was so one of its incidents, I set it down here in its place.

CHAPTER V.

WALK TO SAAS IM GRUND—FEE, AND ITS GLACIER— THE MATTMARK SEE

>   Nature never did betray
> The heart that loved her. 'T is her privilege
> Through all the years of this our life to lead
> From joy to joy : for she can so inform
> The mind that is within us, so impress
>   With quietness and beauty, and so feed
> With lofty thoughts.—WORDSWORTH.

September 4.—Started at 6 A.M. My wife and myself on foot, the little boy on horseback. We walked down the Zermatt valley to Stalden ; and then, turning to the right, ascended the Saas valley. The latter being narrower—so narrow as to bring the opposite mountains very near to you—makes the scenery often more striking than that of the parallel, and wider, valley you have just left. Sometimes the mountain sides are so precipitous, quite down to the torrent, which tumbles, and brawls, along the rocky bottom, that no space is presented even for a cherry or apple-tree. For a great part of the way there is

I

no valley, but only a fissure between the two mountain ranges; and nothing can establish itself in the rifts, and almost on the surface of the rocks, but the larch.

We stopped at a small road-side inn, about an hour and a half from Saas, for luncheon. A German professor and his wife came in for the same purpose. He was a tall, gaunt, study-worn man; she a tough, determined little woman. He recommended Heidelberg (it was not his university) both as a winter residence, and as a place of education. The pair appeared to be, like their country-people generally, honest, earnest, and simple-minded, and in the habit of making the most of their small means without complaining. They were carrying very little besides themselves. We reached Saas im Grund at 12.30. We had been on our legs for six hours. The reason why walking on the level takes more out of one than climbing for an equal number of hours, is not merely that in walking the effort is always the same, but that it is at the same time rapid and continuous; whereas in climbing it is not only varied, sometimes up and sometimes down, but is also deliberate, and often interrupted for a moment or two, while you are looking where to set your foot.

A guide, who was on his way to Saas, overtook us soon after we had left St. Niklaus, and asked permission to accompany our party. He had lately made his first attempt to ascend the Matterhorn.

He had not got to the top, but his having failed to do so was no fault of his. He could speak a little French, and was a good-natured, talkative fellow.

At Saas we put up at Zurbriggen's Hotel. We found the house clean, the people obliging, the charges moderate, and the aspect of things quite unlike—all the difference being on the right side—that of the large Swiss caravansary.

The contrast between Saas and Zermatt is very great. At Zermatt the valley ends, with great emphasis, in a grand amphitheatre of mountains and snowy peaks. At Saas it seems suddenly brought to a close without any objects of interest to look upon. With the mind full of Zermatt, Saas appears but a lame and impotent conclusion. The village, however, is very far indeed from being at the head of the valley. That is to be found at the Monte Moro, five hours further on; and, as it includes the Allalein glacier, the grand scenery of the Mattmark See, and of the Monte Moro itself, it has enough to satisfy even great expectations; such as one has, of course, coming from Zermatt.

September 5.—Went to the Fee glacier with the guide who had joined company with us yesterday. My wife and I walked. The blue boy rode. The path from the village lies across the stream, and up the hill on the west side of the valley. This brings you to a mountain-surrounded expanse of greenest grass, in which lies the village of Fee. The substantial character of the *châlets*, and their tidy air, imply that the inhabitants of the place are pretty well off. At the western extremity of the reclaimed and irrigated meadow is the great Fee glacier. The mounds and ridges of *débris* the glacier has brought down are very considerable. I mean the mounds and ridges that are still naked; for, of course, all that now forms the cultivated valley must equally, only at remoter dates, have been brought down by the same agency. The only difference between the two is that time, and man, have levelled the latter, and enabled it to clothe itself in a vestment of luxuriant grass. This grass it is that has built and peopled the village. In this way human thought and feeling, or rather the multiplication of the thinking and feeling organism, man, is the direct result of the storms, and frosts, that have shattered, and riven, the mountain peaks above; and of the glacier which has transported the fragments to the sheltered valley, where they could be turned to human account; and, in the act of transporting them, so ground and comminuted their constituent particles as to render them capable of maintaining a rich vegetation; and which same glacier is, at this moment, engaged in supplying the irrigating streams, the stimulant of the richness of the vegetation.

The upper part of the naked *debris* overlays large masses of ice. This is very uneven, and full of depressions and cracks, the sides of which are, generally, covered with loose stones, but, sometimes, only with a thin film of mud. A fall upon this combination of ice, pebbles, and slush is the easily attained consequence of inattention to what you are about, and where you are going, while crossing such ground. We had a walk on the glacier; and then, having taken in a fresh supply of materials for keeping up the steam, at a station on one of the *moraine* ridges, which gave us a good view of the contiguous glacier, the overhanging mountains, and the green valley, we returned to Saas in the afternoon.

After dinner I started with our guide—his communicativeness during the two days he had been with us had made us feel as if he were an old acquaintance —for a walk over the Monte Moro, down the Val Anzasca, and over the Simplon, to Brieg. I also took a porter with me, who was to carry my *sac* as far as Macugnaga, from which place the guide was to take charge of it. He would not undertake to carry it where he was known as a guide, for that, he affirmed, would be losing caste. My wrappers I sent from Saas to Brieg by post. The charge was a franc and a half for a great coat and shawl. The latter, of fine wool, four yards in length, and two in width, is less than half the weight of an ordinary travelling rug, and more than twice as serviceable. My portmanteau I had already despatched from Zermatt for Brieg by the same common carriers. The facilities of the Swiss post office for the conveyance of baggage—we found them very convenient—result from the department having absorbed all the diligences. It has thus become the carrier not only of letters, but equally of travellers, and of parcels of all kinds. In fact it seems that in Switzerland you may post anything short of a house. Mistakes appear to be made very seldom; and when they are made you have a responsible office to deal with, whose interest it is to set them right. At Saas the post-master was also the chemist, the doctor, the alpenstock-maker, &c. &c. of the place. Where there are but few people there must be many employments which will not occupy the whole of a man's time, or, singly, support him.

My wife and the little boy accompanied me half of the way to the Mattmark See. Our plan was that they should return to Saas, and on the third day meet me again at Brieg. Soon after they left me I met two well-grown, clean-limbed Englishmen—it is always a pleasure to meet such specimens of one's countrymen—with whom I had a little conversation. I asked them what snow there was on the pass which they had just come over. They told me they had crossed seven snow-fields. The next morning I found only four, and of these two small enough. They could have had no wish to misrepresent; but so fallible is human testimony; and nowhere more so than in Switzerland, where you never find two eye-witnesses giving the same account of the same thing. It is possible, however, that they may have made some *détour* in crossing, and, illogically, answered a question different from the one put to them.

When the path reaches the Allalein glacier the scenery becomes grand. You are again on the visible confines of the ice-and-snow world. On the left side of the glacier you ascend a stiffish mountain. This brings you to the Mattmark See. The path is a little above, and the whole length of, its eastern side. It is carried on a level line along a very rocky descent, a few yards above the water. The humble plants in the narrow rocky strip between the path and the lake were charmingly full of colour, for at this time the leaves of many of them were assuming their rich autumnal tints. At the foot of this narrow strip of shattered rocks, interspersed with highly coloured vegetation, was the unruffled water, looking like polished steel, dark, hard, smooth, and cold. Beyond the water, and rising precipitously from it, towered the rugged, slaty-coloured mountains, capped with white, and streaked in their ravines with snow-drifts and glaciers.

At the further end of the lake stands the Mattmark Inn, exactly where it ought to stand. Further back, you would be disturbed by the feeling that you had not yet seen everything, and so were forming an imperfect conception of the scene. Further on, the scene would, by comparison, be dull. Higher up, the opposite mountain would not look so overpowering, and you would lose the mighty masses of fallen rock, as big as houses, which are close to the inn; and you might also lose the water, which is the distinguishing feature of the scene. As to the inn itself, so far away in the mountains you cannot expect anything very extensive either in the way of structure or of *cuisine*. But you will get here, which is worlds better, a clean house, very obliging people, and all that they can offer for your entertainment—of course without much variety—good of its kind. If you go to Switzerland for what is peculiar to Switzerland, these are the places you should look out for. Large hotels, full of loiterers, among whom there may be perhaps a French count, or even a Russian Prince, may be found elsewhere than in Switzerland, should you think them worth finding. But the very advantage of the Mattmark See Inn, and of other mountain inns like it, is that you will see in them none of this kind of people, while you will have plenty of the grandest mountain scenery, and plenty of mountain work, if that is what you have come for, all around you. From the great hotels you may see the outline of the mountains; but that is a very different thing from being in the midst of the mountains themselves; in the very society and company of the mountains; so that you look at each other face to face, and can make out all their features, and all the components, and the whole colouring, of every feature.

From Saas to the Mattmark See Hotel is three hours and a half. Before turning in I ordered coffee at 3.50 A.M., and told the guide and porter to be ready for a start at 4 A.M.

CHAPTER VI.

OVER MONTE MORO BY MACUGNAGA TO PONTE GRANDE, AND DOMO D'OSSOLA

Creation's heir, the world, the world is mine.—GOLDSMITH.

September 6.—At 3.50 A.M. coffee was ready, but was told that it was not so with the guide and porter. On looking them up, I found them both in bed, and asleep. I was not quite unprepared for this, from something I had been told at Saas about the way in which my friend sometimes spent his evenings. But, having taken a kind of liking to him, I had replied that this would make no difference to me, so long as he was all right during the day. About that I was assured that I need entertain no doubt. The delay, however, caused on this occasion, by his inability to wake of himself at the appointed time, did not, as it happened, amount to much. After a gentle ascent of, if I recollect rightly, about forty minutes, and somewhat beyond the Distel *châlets*, we came to the first snow. It might have been a quarter of a mile across. With nails in your boots, and an alpenstock in your hand, this is almost as easy to walk upon as the path that brings you to it, only, of course, that you cannot walk upon it quite so quickly. Beyond this, the ascent is somewhat stiff up to the summit. Sometimes it is on a ledge of gneiss, with a deep precipice down to the glacier-ravine on your left hand. Another snow-field also has to be crossed here, which lies at an angle of, perhaps, 25° or 30°. The summit of the pass is like a small crater a few yards across. Here my friend, who had been as brisk and talkative as heretofore since we started, called a halt for breakfast. The cold meat and bread were certainly of the driest, and that perhaps encouraged him in the idea that not they, but the liquid with which they were washed down, was the essential part of the repast. Young Andermatten, a name well known in these parts, was now carrying my *sac*. He had met us between the two snow-fields we had passed, and as my porter had some reason for wishing to return to Saas, he had undertaken to supply his place to Macugnaga.

As soon as you leave the summit you begin to descend a ledge of very smooth gneiss, about six or eight feet wide. On your left is a precipice; on your right a broken wall of rock. You go down this for about a hundred yards, and then get off it by a few projecting steps, which have been fixed in the face of the rock. This takes you on to some snow lying at a sharp incline. It would not do to slip on this ledge of gneiss; and, at first, not being used to such paths, that is to say if it is your first pass, you think you must slip. But you take heart when you see your guide walking down it much the same as if he were walking on London pavement. He turns round to see what you are about, and to offer assistance; but that you cannot accept. Still you are glad when it is done. The descent to Macugnaga is, throughout, rough and steep. Ascending it, and with the sun on your back—it faces the south—must be hard work. If it had been a Swiss mountain there would, long ago, have been a good horse-path made to the top.

This is an old and easy pass. Ordinary lungs, ankles, and head, are all that it wants. It was known to, and used by, the Romans. It was for some time occupied by the Saracens, who left their name upon it, as they did names of their own on several peaks and places around it.

As you trudge over the mountain, in the fresh morning air, accompanied by your guide and porter, and with your attention quickened to receive the impressions of the grandeur around you, which you know will hold a place among the most valued and abiding of your mental possessions, you feel as if you were really one of the lords of creation. This feeling would be a wee bit marred, if the eternal mountain had been presumptuously appropriated by some mortal molecule, for then you might be troubled with apprehensions of disturbing, or of being thought likely to disturb, his ibexes and chamois.

I made the Monte Rosa Hotel at Macugnaga at 8.30; that is to say, in four hours from the Mattmark See, excluding the twenty minutes' halt in the little crateriform chamber on the top of the Moro. I now had a breakfast, which, by the grace of 'mine host,' bore a close resemblance to a dinner, for it consisted of a long succession of dishes. This did not come amiss to one who, having been up some time before the sun, had an appetite that took a deal of killing; and 'mine host' had also the grace to charge modestly for what he purveyed bountifully. I found that the inn of the Mattmark See was an off-hand house of his, under the management of his wife. He is besides by profession a guide. He must, therefore, be doubly disposed to regard with favour and sympathy those who do the Monte Moro. I found here a London member of the faculty, who was making Macugnaga his head-quarters for a part of his holiday; and his fuller experiences of the house, and landlord, were all on the right side. The balcony of the hotel commands the best possible view of the upper ten thousand feet of Monte Rosa: its subterranean foundations—the remaining third of its height—are spread out beneath you. You are just at a good distance for taking in the whole of the visible structure—the height, the form, the ravines, the glacier, and the contiguous peaks, with the head of the valley for the foreground. It is a grand, varied, complete, impressive sight.

At 1 P.M. left the Monte Rosa Hotel for Ponte Grande. The guide, who was now also porter, shouldered my *sac* with a jaunty air, and we started at a good pace. My new acquaintance of the hotel joined company for the first mile and a half. At parting we hoped that we should meet again at the Athenæum. At this point you leave the path on *terra firma*, and take to a path, laid on a wooden platform, strewn with sand, which overhangs the brawling Anza. This platform road is curious, and well worth seeing. In some places it is supported by lofty pine poles, which must be fifty or sixty feet high. You hardly understand how support can be found for it in the sheer chasms it occasionally has to be carried along. I have somewhere read that the old Roman road along the bank of the Danube was in places constructed in this fashion, and that the holes cut in the rock, for the bearings of the king-posts and struts, are still visible. This of the Anza is very much out of repair. In some places there are gaps you must step, or jump, over. In others it has been entirely destroyed, and you must make a little *détour* to recover it. For a mile or two, or more, above Ceppo Morelli you quit it altogether, and take to a rocky mule path, which might easily enough be very considerably improved. At Ceppo Morelli is a bridge of one long, slender, much-elevated arch, somewhat in the form a loop caterpillar assumes in walking. Here you return to the left bank; and the carriage road of the Val Anzasca commences. Hitherto we had been walking at a good pace for a rough path; but now the road, having become smooth, invited us to quicken our pace to near four miles an hour. The guide, who had already called two halts, now called them at shorter intervals. He was evidently breaking down. Still he was unwilling to lessen speed. We reached Ponte Grande in a little over four hours. Here is what appeared to be a fairly good hotel. Just before I turned in, the waitress came to inform me that my guide had ordered a carriage, in my name, for the next day. She suspected that all was not right. I asked her to have the carriage counter-ordered, as he was under contract to walk with me over the Simplon to Brieg; and to tell him that I should be off at five o'clock in the morning.

September 7.—Found that the guide's feet were so swollen that he was quite incapable of going any further. The way, I suppose, in which I had understood that he sometimes spent his evenings had been a bad preparation for continuous hard walking, in a valley with very little air, commanded all day by an unclouded sun, and with a dozen, or more, pounds on his back. I was now obliged to leave my *sac*, with instructions that it should be sent on to Domo D'Ossola by diligence; and then started alone. To Pié de Muléra (7½ miles) there is an excellent carriage road. So far you are on the mountain side. From thence to Domo D'Ossola (about 7 miles more) the road is generally on the flat. There was a perfectly clear sky, and no air was stirring; and so I found the latter part of my morning's tramp very warm. Under such conditions one might expect even a water-drinker's feet to swell.

I was in Domo D'Ossola at 12 o'clock. Having breakfasted leisurely and looked over the newspapers in the reading-room of the hotel, I was ready for another ten or twelve miles; and should have done this in the evening had I not thought it better to wait for my *sac*. As it was, I spent the afternoon and night at Domo. As I care little for towns, particularly third or fourth-rate ones, and have seen enough of churches and hôtels de ville, this was an unprofitable waste of time. I amused myself as well as I could with the arrival and departure of the diligences, and with the Italian aspect of things. The hotel was cheerless and lifeless. As soon as a diligence left, everyone about the place suddenly became invisible, just as if they had all sunk into the ground, or melted away into the air. Still, it may be the least unlively house, as things go, in a place so dismally doleful.

To go back then to the valley of the Anza. As soon as you enter it at Macugnaga you see that you are among a more sprightly and joyous people; and are struck with the contrasts between them and the homely Swiss on the other side of the mountains. They are better dressed, and with more attention to effect; particularly the women with their white linen smocks, showing very white beneath the dark jacket, not untouched with colour—this is worn open and sleeveless; and with their more gaudily-coloured kerchiefs on their heads. The dress of the fairer part of creation in Switzerland is somewhat sombre. They make little use of colour, and appear to be attracted most by what will wear best; and, if it may be written, will require least washing. The women in this valley have good eyes. They are not unaware of the advantage, and use them accordingly. Their complexion, too, is clear. That of the Swiss is, generally, somewhat cloudy. Their bearing and air are those of people who are of opinion that the best use of life is to enjoy it. The Swiss seem to regard life as if they were a little oppressed by its cares and labours. Perhaps the conditions of existence on their side of the mountains are so hard, that the people must take things seriously. One respects their laborious industry. There is a kind of manliness in their never-ending struggle against the niggardliness and severity of nature. This, and their forethought, one

K

applauds, only regretting that so much toil should secure so little enjoyment; and should have such humble issues. There is something that pleases, and attracts, in the smiles, and in the greater sense of enjoyment, of the light-hearted Italian.

In the upper part of this valley German is still spoken. Here also it is observable that not nearly so much has been done, as on the Swiss side, to reclaim and irrigate the land. You wish to know whether this is at all attributable to a difference in the distribution and tenure of landed property. You pass several mines: some of gold. The abundance and size of the chesnut-trees are a new feature. You contrast their freely-spreading branches and noble foliage with the formal and gloomy pines, of whose society you have lately had much.

CHAPTER VII.

THE SIMPLON

Julius Cæsar also left behind him a treatise in two books on Analogy (*a department of grammar*); which he composed while crossing the Alps.—SUETONIUS.

September 8.—Last night I had told the head-waiter that I must be off at 5 A.M., and he had replied that it was impossible: that at that hour no one in the hotel would be up; that coffee could not be prepared before six. I, however, gained my point by asking him to set the coffee for me overnight; telling him that I would take it in the morning cold. This proposal appeared to him so uncivilised, that he was confounded by its enormity, and offered no further resistance. I then paid the bill; and was off this morning at the desired time.

As my *sac* had not arrived from Ponte Grande, I left written instructions that, when it turned up—it was due last evening—it should be sent on to Brieg. Thus I had gained nothing by the afternoon I had lost. At Ponte Grande, on the morning after the break-down of my own porter-guide, it was evident that the master of the hotel had conceived the very natural idea of persuading me to take one of his people in that double capacity, or, that failing, to take a carriage. In resentment of this, I had contented myself with putting into my pocket what I should want most during the two following days; and had left the bag, and the rest of what was in it, to chance. I now saw the absurdity of what I had done; for why, in such a matter, should I have taken into consideration, the landlord's scheming, or anything in the world, except my own convenience? My bag, as might have been expected, did not turn up at Brieg. This made me still more conscious of my absurdity. Eventually, however, by the aid of the telegraph and post-office, I recovered it at Interlaken. This I felt I had not deserved.

As you begin to ascend the Simplon, perhaps you will be thinking—at all events you have read remarks of the kind often enough to be reminded of them now— that its road is a line of masonry, carried for forty-four miles over mountains, and through storm and avalanche-swept ravines; that it is one of the mighty works by which man has triumphed over a great obstacle, which nature had placed in his path; that it was constructed for purposes of war and rapine, and for the aggrandizement of an individual, but is now used for the purposes of peace, and for the friendly intercourse of nations ; and that the barrier, which it has practically removed, had its use in those times when it was shielding nascent civilisation from northern barbarism. If so, you will not altogether regret that you are on foot, and alone. This will give you an opportunity for conferring, without irrelevant interruptions, with the *genius loci*, and allow the trains of thought it brings you to unfold themselves, as they will, in your mind : and so, probably, you will feel no want of a *vehiculum*, either literally, or in the metaphorical sense, in which the proverb says the *bonus amicus* is a substitute for it.

This day's walk was very diversified. It began with level ground ; some of it productive, and well cultivated ; some covered with the coarse shingle the torrent stream, which passes through it, has brought down from the mountains. The ascent then commenced through a region of chesnuts and trellised vines. After that came the zone of pines, sometimes lost, and again recovered. At last the scene was compounded of the naked mountain side, the savage ravine, and the blustering torrent, overtopped with rugged crags; these at times capped with snow, and with glaciers between. But even to the summit, as you follow the road, all is not desolation ; for wherever the soil, formed by the weathering of the rock, could be retained, your eye will rest on some little expanse of green turf; or, if the situation be too exposed, and the soil too poor and shallow for turf, it will be clad in the sober mantle of humble Alpine plants.

As I walked along I often noticed how the surface of the fragments of rock lying in the torrent, and their side looking up the stream, were being worn away; while the side looking down, and its upper angle, remained quite unworn. This teaches how the solid rock itself, at the bottom of the torrent, that is to say how its channel, is always being abraded; which means being lowered. While this is going on below, the frosts, and storms, and earthquakes are, at the same time, bringing down the rocks from above. This accounts for the top of the valley, vertically, being very much wider than the bottom. If there had been no frosts, and storms, and earthquakes, the torrent would now be running in a perfectly perpendicular-sided trough, of the same depth as the existing valley—but, then, there would be no valley, only a trough. The valley is wider at the top than at the bottom, because the widening action of frost, storms, and earthquakes has been going on at the top for tens of thousands of years; while it has been going on lower down, with very much less force, only for some hundreds of years. You observe the contrast between the calm majesty of the everlasting mountains and the brawling impatience of the insignificant torrent. The torrent, however, has already set its mark on the mountains; and you see is surely, though slowly, having the best of it. It works, and works incessantly day and night; winter and summer; fair weather and foul. Everything that occurs aids it. The mountain merely stands still to be kicked to death by grasshoppers. But the end of the conflict will be their mutual destruction. The torrent will so far carry away the mountain, that the mountain will no longer be able to feed the torrent. Probably, in the ages preceding the torrent, a glacier, availing itself of some aboriginal facilities in the lay of the ground, commenced the work of excavation, which its successor, the torrent, took up, and has since continued in the line thus prepared for it.

La belle horreur of the gorge of Gondo, its sheer, adamantine, mountain-high precipices, its terrific chasms, its overhanging rocks, its raging torrent, its rugged peaks against the sky, make it the great sight of the ascent. Two bits interested me especially at the moment, and have impressed themselves on my mind more distinctly than the rest. The first was the Fall of the Frosinone. Crashing and roaring, it leaps down from the mountain, a dozen yards or so from the road, under which it passes; beneath a most audaciously conceived and executed bridge, and, immediately, on your left, rushes into the torrent of the Gorge. The road, at once, enters the long tunnel of the Gondo, upon which the bridge abuts. Here is an unparalleled combination of extraordinary and stirring objects. The other is a cascade, a little way off, of a character, in every particular, the opposite of that of the Fall of the Frosinone. It is on the other side of the Gorge. Here there is no ruggedness in the rock. The cleavage of nature has left it, from top to bottom, with a polished surface. Over this almost perpendicular face of the mountain the water glides down so smoothly and so noiselessly that, at night, you would pass it without being aware of the existence of the cascade. The water is as smooth as the rock, and so transparent that you everywhere see the rock through it. It is only, everywhere, equally marked with a delicate network of lines, and bars, of white foam. The effect is precisely that of an endless broad band of lace, rapidly and everlastingly, drawn down the side of the mountain.

The day was bright and warm; and the walk, being all the while against the collar, brought one into the category of thirsty souls. I must have drunk, I believe, twenty times at the little runnels that crossed the road. However heated you may be, and however cold the water, no bad consequences appear to ensue. At 12.30 P.M. I got to the village of Simplon. Here I breakfasted, or dined, for under the circumstances the meal was as much breakfast as dinner; or, rather, it was both in one. As I was now just twenty-two miles from Domo D'Ossola, that is just half way to Brieg, I had thought of sleeping here. Finding the house, however, in possession of a company of strolling Italian players, whose noise and childishness were insufferable, I left the hotel—uninviting enough of itself from the slovenly, dirty look of everything about it; and made for the Hospice, five miles further on. I found it in a sheltered, green depression, on the very summit of the pass. It is a large rectangular massive building, well able to set at defiance even an Alpine winter storm. As it has no stabling, it takes in only those who come on foot.

The Brother, who showed me to my berth, was very young and very good-natured. He brought to me in my room all that I wanted, instead of obliging me to go to the refectory for my supper, where, as it happened, I should have met again the Italian players I had run away from some hours before; for they had followed me on to the Hospice. I might have guessed that they would not have stayed at the inn. Perhaps my alpenstock, and very dusty feet, had some weight with the good man.

September 9.—Was up, and out of my room at 5 A.M. Found no one stirring in the Hospice but a lad and a girl. Both appeared to be about fourteen years of age. For an early traveller to begin the day with, there was plenty of coffee and milk, and of bread and butter, in my room; the remains of the bountiful refection of yesterday evening. On my asking the young people where I was to find some one to whom I might make an acknowledgment for the hospitality I had received, I was told that it was the custom for the visitors to make their offerings in the chapel, putting them in a basin which was shown me behind the door. I left them in the chapel, discussing the amount I had deposited. Having complied with this ceremony, I started for Brieg. As the road was good, and the whole of it downhill, I walked at a good pace, and had completed the sixteen miles at 9.15. There is a short cut by which you may be saved the long *détour* by Berisal, and lessen the distance, as the books say, though I do not believe the books upon this point, to the amount of five miles. I did not look for this short cut, for fear that my attempting to take it might issue in a loss of time. When you don't know the country, the short cut often proves the longest way.

Soon after commencing the descent you come to the galleries, partly excavated in the rock, and partly formed of very massive masonry, through which the road is carried along the flank of the Monte Leone, and across the gorge of Schalbet. These galleries, as well as the Houses of Refuge and the Hospice, shelter the traveller from the storms and avalanches, which are frequent in this part of the pass. The great Kaltenwasser glacier of Monte Leone hangs over them; and the torrent from it slips over the roof of one of the galleries. To find yourself in this way beneath an Alpine torrent, and to look into it, as it dashes by, through an opening in the side of the galleries, will give to some a new sensation. This is the head-water of the Saltine, which joins the Rhone at Brieg. As you pass along this part of the road you have before you the terrific forces, and savagery, of Alpine nature; but you reflect that civilised man has been able, if not to overcome them, yet at all events to protect himself from them. You think that it is something to be a man; or, with less of personal feeling, that civilisation has endowed him with much power. These scenes stir the mind. They enlarge thought, and strengthen will. Below Berisal the torrent of the Gauter, an affluent of the Saltine, is crossed by a massive stone bridge. This is so lofty that it appears a light and airy structure; still it possesses what it requires, a great deal of strength, to enable it to resist the blasts created by the falling avalanches, which are frequent in this neighbourhood. You are surprised at coming so soon in sight of Brieg, and of the valley of the Rhone. You see that you have now completely surmounted the great barrier nature interposed between her darling Italy, where you were yesterday morning, and the hardy North, of which you rejoice to be a child. Perhaps you will think that it was not ill done that you crossed it on foot.

CHAPTER VIII.

BRIEG—THROUGH THE UPPER RHONE VALLEY BY *CHAR* TO THE RHONE GLACIER—HÔTEL DU GLACIER DU RHÔNE

> Happy the man whose wish and care
>   A few paternal acres bound ;
> Content to breathe his native air
>   On his own ground.
>
> Whose herds with milk, whose fields with bread,
>   Whose flocks supply him with attire ;
> Whose trees in summer yield him shade,
>   In winter fire.—POPE.

MY first hour at Brieg was spent in finding the single barber of the place. He was an idle fellow ; and, having it all his own way, was, as it appeared, in the habit of devoting his mornings to society and amusement. His evenings, also, we may suppose, were not allowed, like his business, to run entirely to waste. At last by despatching three little boys, in different directions, to search for him, the finder to be rewarded with half a franc, I succeeded in bringing him back to his razors : mine were in the *sac* I had lost sight of through having lost sight of self. I had breakfasted; had had a little talk with two or three people in the hotel; had looked over the place—no great labour, but the conclusion to which the inspection brought me was that things appear to be better organised in it, and life to be pitched at a higher level, than in places of equal smallness amongst ourselves; had traced the Saltine down to its junction with the Rhone; had had some talk with a woman who was regulating the irrigation of a meadow; and had, having thus exhausted everything local, just retired to my room with a cigar and a book, when the blue boy burst open the door to report himself, like the armies of the old Romans, before he had been expected. When I had left Saas, the calculation had been that my wife and he would not reach Brieg till the evening of this day; and that that might also be the time of my own arrival. We were both before our time. In such calculations, however, it is wise to allow some margin for 'the unforeseen,' and for the imperfections and uncertainties of the human machine. As it happened, had I not lost an afternoon at Domo D'Ossola—I shall for the future in all such deliberations, instinctively, eliminate irrelevant matter—I should have slept in Brieg last night; though, indeed, under the circumstances, there would have been in that no particular gain.

During my absence my wife, and the little man, had made two excursions; one to the Trift glacier with young Andermatten for guide—the youth who in the first hours of the same day had carried my *sac* into Macugnaga, and had then forthwith returned to Saas; and the other, without a guide, to the Mattmark See. Knowing that their thoughts were turned in this direction, I had sent them a note from the Mattmark See, pencilled on the night of the 5th, begging them not to attempt it, as the road was quite too rough and steep, in the latter part, for a child who had shown no great capacity for mountaineering. They did not get my note till they were on the way. My prudence, however, was no match for their enterprise. They managed to get to the Mattmark See Hotel; and, after dinner, to return the same evening to Saas. As the little man was not ten years old, I accept the seven hours they were on foot as an augury of future endurance. I had almost thought, but I ought to have known better, that my note would have deterred them from going; and so, as I tramped along to Ponte Grande, I had not pictured them to myself, as now I did, toiling up the open mountain, and trudging along the lonely shore of the dark Mattmark See, in the very centre of the Alpine world, without another breathing thing in sight.

On the morning of this day (the 9th) my wife had walked from Saas to Visp, fourteen miles. The little boy had ridden. From Visp to Brieg they had come on in the diligence.

September 10.—As it was thirty miles of, we may call it, high road, and that not particularly interesting, from Brieg to the Rhone glacier, for which we were bound, we took a *voiture* for the day. It was a three-horse affair. The driver was an ill-conditioned fellow; but not without some redeeming qualities, for he was the only one of his kind we met with throughout our excursion; and in the afternoon, when *bonne main* had become the uppermost thought in what mind he had, he showed some capacity for the rudiments of civilisation. At Viesch he insisted on stopping for two hours; two hours that were an age, as there was nothing to see there, and nothing that we could do, having just breakfasted at Brieg. It was an aggravation to see at least a dozen one-horse vehicles pass by without one of them halting. At Munster we stopped again, for an hour and a half: but that was for dinner.

This was the first time I had been on wheels since getting upon my own legs at Visp, on August 29. If we had had time enough, it would have been better to have walked this morning to the Belle Alp, giving to it one day; then on to the Eggischhorn, for the great Aletsch glacier; two days more: and thus reaching the Rhone glacier on the fourth day. But as we could hardly have spared the time for this, we were satisfied with what we did. To refuse to take a carriage on a carriage road, when much time is saved by taking it, and every object along the road can be seen as well from a carriage as on foot, is the pedantry of pedestrianism, which sacrifices the substance of one's object for useless consistency.

In the upper part of the Rhone valley there are considerable expanses of good grass land, particularly about Munster; and the villages are numerous, and close together. Each of these villages, as seen from a little distance, is a cluster of *châlets*, without any visible internal spaces, and without any apparent differences in their dimensions, or structure. They have no suburbs; there is no shading off; the bright green meadow is not gradually lost in the dark brown village. The houses do not gradually thin out in the fields. There are no fields; no detached houses. There is nothing but the expanse of grass, and these clusters of *châlets*, each like a piece of honeycomb laid upon it; and as distinct from each other as so many communities of bees. Each village looks as if it were something that had dropped from heaven upon the grass; or like a compact, homogeneous excrescence upon the grass—a kind of Brobdingnagian fungus. There is, however, one exception to the general uniformity of the excrescence, and that is the church tower. It stands above the rest, just as its shaft would, if the Brobdingnagian fungus were turned upside down.

Here you have, apparently without disturbing elements, as perfect a picture, as could now be seen, of the old rationale of religion; that it is a power among men, equally above all, interpreting to all their moral nature, and proclaiming the interpretation to all with an authoritative voice; and obliging all, by its constant authoritative iteration, to receive the proclamation; and to allow its reception to form within themselves, even if they were such as by nature would have been without conscience, the ideas and sentiments requisite for society. You see that this Arcadian application of the function of religion may have been completely, and undisturbedly realised, in times past, in such isolated and self-contained villages; and that you are at the moment looking upon one in which it is still being realised to some extent. But you, who belong to the outside world, and know it, too; its large cities, its wealth, its poverty, its estranged classes, its mental activity, its social and controversial battle-shouts, its pæans of short-lived triumph, its cries of agonising defeat, its individualism, are aware that the day for such an exhibition of religion is gone by. Your religion, if you are religious, will be in the form, and after the kind, needed now in that outside world. It will have stronger roots, that seek their nutriment at greater distances; a firmer knit stem, such as a tree will have that has grown up in the open, exposed to many gales; and more wide-spreading branches, such as those far-travelling roots, and that firm-knit stem, can alone support. And this will enable you to under-

L

stand, and, if you do understand, will save you from despising, the religion of the Alpine village before you: for you will find that it is the same as your own, only in embryo.

At Oberwald, three and a half miles from the Rhone glacier, the road leaves the grassy valley, and begins to ascend the zig-zags on the mountain-side. We here found the inclination to leave the carriage, and walk, irresistible. This road, which is carried over the Furca Pass to Andermatt, is a grand achievement, for which the country, and those who travel in it, have to thank the modern, more centralised and democratised government. To it also their thanks are due for the new coinage, the most simple in the world, whereas the old cantonal coinages it superseded were the most confusing, and the worst; for the postal arrangements, which are very good; for the telegraph; and even for the railways. And, furthermore it must be credited with many advances, and improvements, that have been made in the Swiss system of education.

The Rhone glacier is a broad and grand river of ice. As it descends from the mountains on a rapid incline you see a great deal of it from below, and are disposed to regard it as worthy to be the parent of a great historic river. The Rhone, however, itself issues from it, at present, in a very feeble and disappointing fashion. It slips out from beneath the ice so quietly, and inconspicuously, that you might pass by it, as doubtless many do, without observing it. It steals off, as if it were ashamed of its parentage; of which, rather, it might well be proud.

A word about the Hôtel du Glacier du Rhône. It has plenty of pretension; but I never passed a night in a house I was so glad to leave in the morning. Nowhere did one ever meet with such a plague of flies, flies so swarming, and so persecuting; and nowhere did one ever meet with such revolting stenches. What produces the stenches is what produces the flies; that is want of drainage, and the non-removal of unclean accumulations. At first, on account of the stench which pervaded the gallery—it was that of the first and chief floor, I refused to take the room I was shown to; and only, after a time, consented on the assurance that this matter could, and should be set right. This assurance was utterly fallacious; for, though I kept my window wide open, from the time I entered the room till I left it, I soon sickened, and was afflicted with uninterrupted nausea throughout the whole night. Want of proper drainage, the cause of these horrors, is very common in Swiss hotels. Their pretentious character, which, with many thoughtless people, atones for much, ought, on the contrary, to intensify one's sense of such shameful neglect. The larger the house is the larger are the gains of the landlord, and the greater is the number of people exposed to the mischief. I do not at all join in the cry against the rise in the charges of the monster hotels of Southern Switzerland. Landlords, like other people, have a right to charge what they can get, when the commodity they deal in is much in demand. But, as their charges are certainly remunerative, there can be no reason for forbearing to denounce manifest and disgraceful disregard of necessary sanitary arrangements. I heard the next morning from one, who spoke from that day's personal experience, that matters were no better at the neighbouring hotel of the Grimsel Hospice. Strange is it that man should be so careless about poisoning the very air nature has made so pure!

CHAPTER IX.

WALK OVER THE GRIMSEL BY THE AAR VALLEY, HELLE PLATTE, FALLS OF HANDECK, TO MEIRINGEN

> These are Thy glorious works, Parent of good ;
> Almighty, Thine this universal frame,
> Thus wondrous fair ; Thyself how wondrous, then !
> Unspeakable, Who sitt'st above the heavens
> To us ihvisible, or dimly seen
> In these Thy lowest works.—MILTON.

September 11.—We were off at 6 A.M. for a long day over the Grimsel Pass to Meiringen. As usual, my wife and I on foot, and the little man on horseback. You begin the ascent of the mountain immediately from the hotel. It is stiff walking all the way to the top, which is reached in about an hour. The height above the sea is somewhat more than 7,000 feet. On the side of the mountain the most conspicuous plant is the Rhododendron, the rose of the Alps. On the summit of the pass is a dark tarn. The mephitic Hospice, about three fourths of a mile off, is 700 feet below. Soon after you begin the descent you come upon indications of former glacier action in polished slabs of gneiss all around you. On your right is a rugged glacier, among still more rugged pinnacles of rock. Before you and to the left, is a world of snowy mountains, of which you catch some glimpses. After a few yards of descent from the Hospice the path strikes the Aar, fresh from its exit from the upper and lower Aar glaciers. It then turns to the right along the margin of the torrent: the torrent and the path passing side by side through a narrow defile, overtopped, right and left, with precipitous mountains. After a time the path leaves the margin of the torrent, having first been carried over it by a narrow stone bridge. Everywhere you find indications of the great height to which the glaciers reached in some remote epoch. Among these are several instances of deep horizontal lines, graven along the apparently perpendicular face of the mountain, at a height of even 2,000 feet above the valley. In a place called *Helle Platte*, or the Open Plain, the path is carried over what was formerly the bed of the glacier; the gneiss still retaining the polish that was given to its surface so many millenniums ago. This extends for about a quarter of a mile, the interstices, between the mighty slabs of gneiss being filled with fringes and patches of stunted Rhododendrons, and of the Pinus Pumilio, a spreading dwarf pine, that does not reach more than three or four feet from the ground; but which, notwithstanding its diminutive size, conveys to you, far more impressively than its lofty congeners, the idea of great age. This scene surrounded by naked mountain masses, as rugged as adamantine, stirs the mind deeply. The effect culminates as you pass the bridge, beneath which the torrent of the Aar roars and dashes along its rock-impeded channel. No animal life is seen, with the one exception of a multitude of butterflies, glancing to and fro in the clear warm sunshine, like winged flowers. Your thought is interested by the contrast between their feeble fragile beauty and the force and savagery of surrounding nature.

The way in which I saw that the Aar had cut its channel through the gneiss suggested to me the inquiry, whether what had enabled it to do this was not the fact that the pebbles and broken rock the torrent brought down were gneiss, so that it was gneiss which it had to dash against the sides and bottom of its channel. Perhaps torrent-borne fragments of gneiss may widen and deepen a gneiss channel as effectually as fragments of lime-stone may a lime-stone channel.

At eleven miles from the Rhone glacier you reach Handeck: a small expanse of greenest Alpine meadow, intermixed with pine-forest, and surrounded with dark craggy mountains. Here we called a halt for luncheon, and a cigar. It was a bright, airy day; one to be for ever remembered. Many travellers came and went; some facing up, some down the pass.

Fortunately this charming spot has not yet been disfigured by a staring stone hotel. The suave landlord, and expectant porter, have not yet invaded it. But I am afraid that they cannot be far off. At all events for the present, may it long remain so! you have the wooden *châlet*, with its low panelled reception room, innocent of gilding and of paint; the green rock-strewn turf coming up to the door; and the bench along the wall outside. You can here get a mutton chop that has not been first passed through a bath to make *potage* for yesterday's visitors, and then, for you, had its impoverishment thinly disguised by having been dipped into a nondescript *sauce piquante*.

This charming halting-place is enriched with far the best waterfall in Switzerland—the Fall of the Handeck. The Staubbach, Byron's magniloquence nevertheless, and the rest of them, are only overflows of house-gutters. There, where they are, just at the first stage of the watershed of Europe, they can be accepted as being very much what they ought to be; but one cannot be impressed with them as waterfalls. Here, however, is something of quite a different kind: not so much from the volume of the falling water, as from its character, and the point of view from which it is seen. Two or three hundred yards below the *châlet* the Aar is chafing along its clean rock-channel, strewn with boulders as large as houses; on a sudden it takes a leap, of about two hundred feet, into a dark, appalling, iron-bound chasm. Precisely at the point, where it takes this leap, the Handeck, coming blustering down on the left, at a right angle to the Aar, takes the same leap. The two cataracts are mingled together, midway in the chasm. A wooden bridge has been thrown over the falls. You stand upon this, and see the hurrying torrents dashing themselves into the deep chasm below you. You are half stunned by their angry roar. You observe that they have no power to undermine, and wear away, the granite against which they are dashing, and breaking themselves. The frail bridge vibrates under your feet. Fortunately you are looking down the fall instead of up, and this, by engendering an irrational sense of the possibility of your slipping into it, heightens the effect. For some hours about midday—we were there at that time—it is crowned with the prismatic bow.

Here my wife took a horse for the rest of the day, being too ill of the Hôtel du Glacier du Rhône to walk any further. After some miles the savage character of the scenery began to relent. This mitigation went on increasing, till at last we found ourselves crossing the emerald meadows of Guttanen—a village of *châlets*. Next came the little town of Imhof. Here an hotel, and a brewery, a good road, and the slackened pace of the Aar made it evident that we were out of the mountains; and the plain at Meiringen was soon reached. This was a walk of about twenty-six miles.

As all the hard work came in the first hour, it was a very much easier day than the twenty-seven miles up the southern side of the Simplon.

As we were in Meiringen by 4.20 P.M., there was time for a walk up the hill, close to the hotel, to see the Falls of the Reichenbach. I was glad to find the little man ready to accompany me, for he had been so silent all day that I had been thinking he was fatigued, or not well. When we had got some way up the hill we met a Frenchman coming down, who told us that a toll would soon be levied upon us ; his comment upon the fact being that we should have to pay for looking at the mountains, if it could in any way be managed. Regarding this toll as a piece of extortion, and not at all caring to see the fall, we returned to the hotel. If I had thought it really worth going to see, I should, acting on the wisdom I had purchased at Ponte Grande, have eliminated from consideration, though perhaps with a growl, the meanness and rapacity of the demand, as irrelevant matter, and have gone on ; but it was getting late, and we thought we had seen enough of the fall from the road as we were entering Meiringen.

CHAPTER X.

CHAR TO INTERLAKEN—WALK OVER THE WENGERN ALP
TO GRINDELWALD

> I love not man the less, but nature more
> From these our interviews.—BYRON.

September 12.—This morning we went by *char* from Meiringen to Interlaken, along the northern side of the Lake of Brienz. Again, if we had had time, it would have been better to have walked along the southern side, putting up for the night at Giesbach. While stopping at the town of Brienz to bait the horse, we visited some of the wood-carving shops, in one of which we found a school for indoctrinating children in the mysteries, not of the three R's, but of this trade, which is the great industry of the place: everybody here being engaged in it. The three main staples of Southern Switzerland are this wood-carving, cheese-making, and hotel-keeping. With the latter we must connect the dependent employments of the guides and porters, and of those who let out horses and carriages. I know not how much of the cheese is sent out of the country in exchange for foreign commodities, but pretty nearly the whole of the carved wood, and of the hotel accommodation, is exchanged for foreign cash.

This morning I witnessed the following scene. A practical man—I took him for one, who had struck oil—was leaving the hotel. A porter, assuming an expectant air, takes up a position at the door of the hotel. The practical man addresses him in a firm tone, 'Now, sir, tell me everything, you have done for me beyond your duty to the hotel.' A look of blankness comes over the porter's face, and he steps aside. The practical man, with the look of one who has discharged a lofty duty, steps into his carriage. I do not record this for imitation.

Interlaken, which we reached early in the day, is a town of hotels and *pensions*. We were at The Jungfrau, which commands an excellent view of the famous mountain from which it takes its name. The view from this point is much improved by its comprising two intermediate distances in two ranges of hills, which do not at all interfere with the dominant object, but rather set off to advantage its snowy summits and flanks. The Jungfraublick, a large new hotel, on a spur of the nearest hill, is better situated, for it is out of the town; and, being elevated above the lakes, commands several good views. The majority of the visitors at our hotel were Germans:

quiet, earnest, and methodical, they appeared to be regarding travelling, sight-seeing, and life itself, scientifically.

Interlaken, being situated on low ground, between two high ranges of mountains, at no great distance from each other, is, on a quiet sunny day, a very oven for heat. It has, however, in its main street some very umbrageous lofty walnut-trees. They are the survivors of what was once, and not many years ago, a grand unbroken avenue.

September 13.—Started early in a carriage for Lauterbrunnen, where we left it, with orders that it should be taken round to Grindelwald, there to be ready for us the next morning. At Lauterbrunnen we put the blue boy on horseback, and began the ascent of the Wengern Alp. People go up this mountain for the purpose of getting the most accessible, nearest, and best view of the Jungfrau, Mönch, and Eiger. As you turn to the left to ascend the mountain, you regret that you are not going up the valley, which you see would lead you up among glaciers and snowy peaks; or that you are not taking the path to the right, which you see would carry you over, and above the Staubbach, and you know would give you grand views of the snow-world. The path you are taking you take in faith, for it does not, from what is in sight, give any indications of what is in store for you; before, however, the day is done, you will have reason enough for being satisfied with the choice you had made ; or which, perhaps, had been made for you.

At first the ascent is very stiff, and a good test of lungs and legs. This lasts for about an hour. Then comes a reach of easy work among upland meadows and forest. The work, however, again stiffens ; but one is cheered by the nearness of the Jungfrau, and, occasionally, by the thunder of an avalanche, falling from its sides. You are now above the forest, and on the coarse sedgy turf; and, if you please, you may sit down, and light your cigar, giving as your reason, that you wish to contemplate the view, and listen to the avalanches. It would, however, be better to go on at once to the hotel, which is not far off. This was what we were virtuous enough to do. The ascent occupied a little under four hours. We had luncheon at the hotel. It is on the edge of the ravine, on the opposite side of which rises, almost perpendicularly, the mighty Jungfrau. Though it must be two miles off, it seems so near that you fancy you might almost touch it with your hand. The dark, slate-coloured rock, and the snow, are in excellent contrast. The vast chasm below you, and the cold, hard, silent cliffs before you, the silence frequently broken on bright, warm days—and the day we were there was as bright and warm as could be—by the reverberation of the falling avalanches—there are no small, or insignificant objects in sight to mar the effect—are the elements of an Alpine scene you are glad to think you will carry away impressed on your memory. You are now content that the path on the right, up to Mürren, has been left for another day. As you watch the avalanches gliding down the ravines, and shot over the precipices, in streams of white dust, for the first fall or two shiver them into minute fragments, you are puzzled to know what it is that makes the thunder—what the noise is all about, the process being so smooth and regular.

We allowed ourselves an hour and a half for mental photography and for luncheon—mine was a basin of rice-water, for I had not yet recovered from the Hôtel du Glacier du Rhône. We then again took up our staves, and set our faces towards Grindelwald. In half an hour from our inn, we came to a second, on the summit of the Col. The descent immediately commences. This is not nearly so steep as the ascent we had just accomplished. It requires three hours. The path passes through the forest of death-struck pines Byron mentions in his journal. Not many remain. Of these some are quite, some are almost dead. It was composed of the Pinus Cembra. The malady which is destroying it may perhaps have been engendered by a local change of climate; or some other circumstance may have prevented the young plants from establishing themselves; as, for instance, want of shelter, from too much of the forest having been cut at the same time. I mention this because I observed in exposed situations in the Rocky Mountains—it was so above Nevada City, on the road to Georgetown—wherever the forest had been entirely cleared away, the young pines came up in myriads, but all died off, either withered by the droughts of summer, or by the bleak winds of winter: of course neither of these causes could have afflicted the tender nurselings, had the old forest been standing.

The descent, like that to Virgil's Avernus, is easy, but, unlike that into the Vale of Years, has a charming prospect; for the valley of Grindelwald, with its meadows, corn-fields, and *châlets*, is all spread out before you, like a map. It is a sight which awakens thought and touches the heart. You see that a good breadth of land has been reclaimed, where nature was so hard and adverse. How much labour has been expended in burying the stones, and bringing the soil to the surface, and in irrigating those many, now bright, smooth meadows! How much thought and care is, day by day, bestowed on every little plot of that corn and garden ground, in the hope of getting a sufficiency of the many things that will be needed in the long winter! How much talk is there, every evening, in every household, about the way in which things are going on, and about what has to be done! A shoulder-basket must now be made for little Victor, and little tasks must be found for him, proportioned to his little strength, that he may, betimes, learn to labour; and something must be found, too, for the old grandame to do, that she may not come to feel that she is only burdensome. Some garden or dairy product, a little better than common, they may have in their humble stores, must be reserved for the *fête*, now not far off. Wilhelm, who many a mother in the valley wishes may be her son-in-law, and who of late has been more thoughtful than was his wont, hearing the *fête* mentioned, is reminded of the *edelweiss* he had gone in search of, and found on the Eiger, that he may have its tell-tale flower, on that day when all hearts will be glad and open, to offer to Adeline. I suppose the fat Vale of Aylesbury, where purple and fine linen are not wanting, and there is sumptuous fare every day, has its poetry; but so, also, has the hard-won valley of Grindelwald, where home-spun is not unknown, and every man eats the bread of carefulness.

We put up at the Aigle, a new hotel, with three or four *dépendances*, at the further end of the village. Grindelwald is not of the compact order of Swiss villages; indeed, it is almost a town; at all events, it is lighted with gas. It straggles along the main road for about three quarters of a mile; to those coming from Lauterbrunnen all uphill. It abounds in hotels. After a hard day—not the Wengern Alp, but the Hôtel du Glacier du Rhône, had made it hard—it appeared a gratuitous, almost a cruel, infliction to have to pass so many doors that stood open invitingly, with more than usual persuasiveness, and to trudge on, and up, in the hope of reaching the end of the place, which, under the circumstances, seemed like the Irishman's bit of string, which had had its end cut off. But to those who will persevere, even the street of Grindelwald will be found to have an end; and one, too, that is worth finding, for it brings you to a pleasantly situated, and well-kept inn, where you can get a chicken that has not been detained in the bath an unconscionable time. What has been disagreeable in travelling we soon forget, but my recollections of the Aigle of Grindelwald remain.

There are, as I just said, many hotels in the place; but as there are also six thousand cows in the valley, not travellers, but cheese must be its main reliance. It has another industry in ice, which is cut in blocks out of the glacier, and sent as far even as Paris. The price returned for this is one of the rills of the stream of wealth, which railways are pouring into Switzerland, or enabling it to collect for the outside world. Two great glaciers come down into the village from the two sides of the Mettenberg, which here has the Eiger on its right, and the Wetterhorn on its left.

We had been on the tramp to-day, excluding the halt for luncheon, eight hours. With the exception of not more than five minutes on the little man's horse, my wife did the whole of it on foot, stepping out briskly even to the long-sought end of Grindelwald.

CHAPTER XI.

INTERLAKEN AGAIN—CHAR UP THE VALLEY OF THE KANDER
—WALK OVER THE GEMMI, SLEEPING AT SCHWARENBACH

> —rather—
> To see the wonders of the world abroad
> Than, living dully sluggardized at home,
> Wear out thy youth with shapeless idleness.—SHAKESPEARE.

September 14.—Returned early in our *voiture* to Interlaken. From the tramping point of view, the right thing to have done in the afternoon would have been to have ascended one of the ranges of mountains, which shut in Interlaken on the right and left. But it was fair that the little man should have his turn, and his heart was all for the railway, the steamer, and the Lake of Thun: and so we went by rail, and boat, to Thun and back. The railway, with its smart carriages, some of them two stories high, is only a mile or two in length, from Interlaken to its port on the lake, and is a mere toy. As to the sail on the lake, it supplies enough for the eye to feed upon. The chief objects on the south side are the Niesen and the Stockhorn; the two mountains which form the porch of the valley of the Kander, up which lies the road to the Gemmi. The boat was very crowded with people who were going northward; the greater part of them to Berne, the rail for which commences at Thun. About Thun what interests one most at this season, as things are seen from the water, are the gardens of some of the houses on the edge of the lake. The little man, from familiarity with threshing machines and agricultural implements, has a strong turn for machinery; hence the attraction for him of the railway and steamboat. On board the latter he poked about, looking into everything, as if he were taking the opportunity to inspect some of his own property.

'This was a day, which, to its end, was given up to the young gentleman, for in the evening he would have us go to the Cursaal to see a display of fireworks. They were pretty good. The best thing was the illumination of a copious jet of water, which was thrown up to the height of about a hundred feet, and fell very much broken and dispersed; the upward rush, and the falling drops, reflecting a powerful red light, which, screened to the spectators, was burnt in front of the fountain. The shrubberies, and trees, all about, were at times illuminated, successively, with red, blue, and white lights: this was meant to be weird and spectral.

September 15.—It was Sunday. We went twice to

the English service. On both occasions the preacher was extemporary. He was fluent and imaginative. Fluency, and imaginative power (I say this without intending a reference to the sermons we heard this day), if entirely trusted to at the moment of speaking, and not kept under the control of previously matured thought, will generally run away with a preacher, and lead him into making inconsequential, and unguarded statements. And if he is, besides, a man of some miscellaneous reading, it is not improbable that much of it will be presented to his audience in an undigested form, and not unfrequently rather incongruously. In short, all that he says is likely to be what Shakespeare calls unproportioned speaking.

While we were at Interlaken, the moon was approaching the full. Both evenings we watched it passing over the peaks of the Jungfrau. The snow, however, had none of the deadly white, I had expected it would have had when seen by moonlight. But the moon was beyond the mountain, and so almost all the snow on our side was in the shade.

September 16.—Were to have started at 6 A.M. for the Valley of the Kander, on our way to the Gemmi: through the dilatoriness, however, of the *voiturier* we had some difficulty in getting off by 6.25. And this was not his only lapse; for, an hour after a forty minutes' halt for breakfast, he insisted on halting again, for two hours more, at a roadside inn, where he, and his horse, were baited; both probably at our expense, for he had brought nothing with him for either. As these stoppages are, sometimes, not so much needed for the horse, as the result of arrangements between innkeepers and drivers, which become profitable to them through what is extracted from you, it would, perhaps, not be a bad plan to make it understood beforehand, that your payments will, to some extent, depend on the time at which the driver may bring you to your destination.

The road is, at first, along the lake. At the place, where it makes an angle, and turns its back upon the lake, we breakfasted. The inn looks upon the lake. The house itself is not bad; but what is best about it is the feeling it gives rise to that you have escaped from the crowding, the bad smells (the Jungfrau was free from these), and the pretensions, of a monster hotel, where everything is in disagreeable contrast to surrounding nature; the effects of life in the former at every turn counteracting and marring the effects of the latter.

A geologist should follow the new channel by which the Kander 150 years ago was taken into the lake. He will be interested by an inspection of the large delta, at the mouth of its new outlet, formed by the vast amount of *débris* the torrent-stream has since brought down. Formerly it ran parallel to the lake; and joined the Aar below it, in this part of its course keeping a great deal of land in a marshy condition. All this has now been reclaimed.

The scenery of the valley is interesting. From Frutigen—it was here that our two hours' halt had been called—to Kandersteg, at the foot of the Gemmi, is eight miles. The last half of this my wife and I walked.

At Kandersteg we dined; and having placed the little man, and the baggage, on horses, we began the ascent at 3.30. The road is in excellent repair. For the first hour and a half it is stiff walking through a pine forest. The views of the valley of the Kander, and of the mountains, are good. The road is then, for some distance, taken horizontally along the side of the mountain, again through the pine forest. Between the clean stems of the trees you look down, on your left, into the barren, and truly Alpine, Valley of Gasteren. At first it is a rocky gorge; and then it opens into an expanse of level, pale grey sand, and small shingle, through which you can make out, from above, the glacier stream passing in several small channels. The forest is succeeded by an open level of poor mountain pasture and rocky ground. On the left of this are the peaks of the Altels, and of the Rinderhorn, with snow-fields and glacier. You then begin to ascend again through a scene that is the very grandeur of desolation. There is no vegetation; nothing that has life. It appears as if the mighty fragments of dark rock, with which the whole is covered, had been rained down from heaven in its wrath, and had completely buried out of sight everything that might once have struggled up here for life, and even whatever could have supported life. This mountain in ruins, this wrack of rocks, brings you to the Schwarenbach inn. It stands on the edge of a crateriform depression, in what appears at the time, and from the spot, to be the summit of the mountain. This depression terminates, on the right, in a grand mountain amphitheatre.

The inn is precisely what it ought to be; small, without any pretension, and without any artificial *entourage*. The people, too, who keep it are most ready, and obliging. This is just the sort of place one would like to make one's head-quarters, for a few days, for excursions from it among the surrounding summits, and for familiarising oneself with the spirit of the mountains.

September 17.—Started a little after 5 A.M., that we might see the sun rise from the summit of the pass. Overnight I had been roused out of my first sleep by a loud, hurried knocking against the thin partition, that separated my room from my wife's, accompanied by repeated calls to get up at once. I lighted a match, and looked at my watch. It was just 11 o'clock. At 4.30 A.M. the knocking was again heard : but this time it came from the opposite side of the partition.

The morning was very cold. The blue boy, and the luggage, were on horseback ; my wife, and I, on foot. The ascent continued for about two miles further. For the first mile the path takes you by two or three more crater-like depressions, similar to the one on the edge of which the inn stands. You then come to a dark mountain lake, fed by the glacier of the Wildstrubel, at the southern end of it. It is another scene of awful desolation. You are surprised at observing that the detrital matter, neither of the glacier, nor of the environing mountains, has in the least degree diminished the size of the lake. It seems to-day to be just the same, in size and form, that it must have been thousands of years ago. The crest of the ridge is reached a little beyond the lake. The sight that here bursts upon you is grand indeed. The eye passes over the valley of the Rhone—that, however, is not yet visible—and rests on the long series of snowy peaks, which you know are the finials of the barrier ridges that separate Switzerland from Italy—the Michabel, the Weisshorn, the Matterhorn, the Dent d'Heréns, the Dent Blanche. On this morning they all stood clear of cloud. While close, on our left, just to show us how near we were to losing the view, a dense mist was streaming over the mountains, like a turbid, aerial river, flowing uphill

Nothing could be grander; the rocky peaks around us, the snowy peaks before us, and the river of cloud rolling by us. We had reached the right point at the right moment.

Having impressed the view on our minds, as 'a possession for ever,' we began the descent. The little man got off his horse, for the descent can only be made on foot; at all events it always has been, since the fatal accident, caused by the stumbling of her horse, which here befel the Comtesse d'Arlincourt in 1861. The luggage, too, was now readjusted, and more tightly braced up on the baggage horse.

Among those who keep to beaten paths the descent of the Gemmi is the crowning glory of their excursion. This it is that awakens within them most the sensations of awe and wonder. And there is much to justify these feelings. As you come down the pass, you cannot but be surprised at the boldness, ingenuity, and perseverance of those who projected, and made it. And, perhaps, your surprise will be heightened when, on getting to the bottom, and looking up at the sheer precipice of some thousands of feet of hard rock, you find that you are unable to make out a trace of the path you have just been descending. A fissure in the perpendicular face of the mountain just made it conceivable that a series of zig-zags might be carried up to the top. And this was what the engineer attempted, and succeeded in doing. Originally, many of the zig-zags were nothing more than grooves in the face of the rock, just sufficient to give foothold to a pedestrian. During the last century, however, they have been widened into grooves that admit, with perfect safety, the passage of a packhorse with his burden. The external wall of a house may be ascended by a staircase applied to it; and so may the perpendicular face of a mountain, two or three thousand feet high. And it will come to the same thing if the staircase is, in some places, let into the face either of the house, or of the mountain wall. The motive of the formation of the pass was to save a *détour* of some days in getting from the neighbourhood of Thun and Interlaken to the Valais. I suppose it was worth making as a saving of time and labour. But, be that as it may, it impresses itself on the mind as a never-to-be-forgotten passage of one's Alpine travel. The blue boy skipped down it, like a chamois, far in advance of everybody; a guide, of course, being with him. My wife insisted on going down at the head of the rest of the party, on the plea that she was incapable of going behind. I took the position assigned me, with a little hug of myself at the conceit, the benefit of which, however, at the time I kept to myself, that those, who can go as well behind as before, must be twice as clever as those who can go before only.

CHAPTER XII.

LEUKABAD—AIGLE

> The life of man is as the life of leaves,
> Which, green to-day, to-morrow sears, and then
> Another race unfolds itself to run
> Again the course of growth and of decay :
> So waxes, and so wanes the race of man.—HOMER.

AT a little after 8 A.M. we entered Leukabad, having been out three hours from Schwarenbach. I was content that both our *personnel* and our *matériel* were safe, plus the ineffaceable impression on our minds of the pass itself.

Having breakfasted—it is pleasant to have lived so much before breakfast—we sallied forth to look at the town and the baths. There are several hotels in the place, and they were all pretty well tenanted. Still the aspect of things was not lively. There was none of the stir you observe among the Alpine people at such places as Chamouni and Zermatt; nor was there any of the obtrusive bigness, and of the staring newness of the hotels almost everywhere, which give you to understand very clearly that, at all events, a great deal of business is being done. Here nothing was new, and everything was faded. The names over the hotels and shops had been there many a day; and the hotels and shops themselves made one think of a dead forest covered with lichens and moss, the lichens and moss being at least half dead also. People moved about so noiselessly that you looked to see if their feet were muffled; saying nothing to each other, and having nothing to say. The place was as dumb as it was faded. We saw an old man washing old bottles, of a by-gone form, at an old fountain, into and out of which the water was feebly dribbling, as if it had nearly done coming and had nowhere to go. He was the only person we saw doing anything, and he did it as if he thought there was no use in doing it. Those who were taking the baths were oppressed with a consciousness that they were getting no good from them; and that they were doing it only because something must be attempted. Their despondency had an air of obstinacy that would not be comforted, deep and silent; like that of people who have just found out that the foundations on which they have long been building great expectations, are all a delusion,—either a figment of their own, or a tradition from times when such things were not understood— and who have not yet come to think that the world may still have something else for them to turn to. At

12 o'clock the *voiturier* we had engaged to take us to Sierre, came up to the door of the hotel, with his worm-eaten vehicle and his worn-out horses. But he came in so mute and spectral a fashion—anywhere else he would have announced himself with a little final flourish and crack of his whip—that we were not for some time aware of his arrival. It was a relief when he lighted his cigar, for that was the first indication of life we had seen in the place.

On the road to Sierre we passed through dust enough to bury Leukabad—a ceremony which it would be as well should not be deferred any longer. And, if Sierre had been put on the top of it, there would still have been some to spare.

This dusty drive enhanced the pleasantness of recalling our late mountain walks. We had now completed the circuit of the great ice-field of the Bernese Oberland, which is more than 100 square miles in extent, and is supposed to be the largest in Europe. Its boundaries, all of which we had traced, are the Valais, the Grimsel, the Valley of the Aar, and the Gemmi. We had had a near or more distant view of all its chief snowy peaks, but had nowhere crossed any part of the snow-field itself. That, perhaps, may be the work of another day, when the blue boy will be old enough, and the rest of the party not yet too old, for such work; for those who are not up to Peaks, either of the first or second class, may still graduate as Pass-men by crossing the ice-fields between the Peaks.

Another possible arrangement for the work of the two last days would have been to have ascended the Niesen, at the foot of which we had passed yesterday morning. This would have obliged us to have slept at Kandersteg instead of, as we did, at the top of the Gemmi. The ascent of the Niesen, even for such a party as was ours, would have been easy enough; and the views from it are said to be very good. In that case, however, we should have had to do the Gemmi at one stretch. Our loss would have been sleeping at Kandersteg, and not at the Schwarenbach, and the abandonment of our chance of a good sunrise from the summit of the Pass; though that was a chance which, as it happened, was worth nothing to us; for, in such perfectly fine, and singularly clear weather as we had, the sun rises and sets without those glories of colour which require haze and clouds for their reflection.

As to weather, which is the first, the second, and the third requisite in such an expedition, we had scarcely seen a cloud during our three weeks' tramp. Up to the day before I got on my legs at Visp it had been an unusually wet and cold season. During the night I was at the Simplon Hospice it rained a little. That was the only shower that fell, where I was, during the whole time we were out. The quarter of an hour's snow on the Riffel was merely the passage of a stray bit of mountain scud. The sun, throughout, had shone so brightly that some of its brightness had been reflected from the world outside upon the world within. Almost every party of travellers in Switzerland, this year, we met with had a very different account to give of the weather they had encountered. When good luck is pleased to come, it must fall to some one; and this year it fell to us.

So ended the second act of our little family excursion. The scene of the first had been the Valleys of Zermatt and Saas, with my intercalated tramp over the Monte Moro, through the Val Anzasca, and over the Simplon. I can, with a safe conscience, recommend the precise route we took to any family party, constituted at all as ours was. The time occupied, from first to last, was exactly three weeks; and three weeks they were, which we look back upon as well spent. It had no difficulties, and enough of interest and variety. As to the cost, I can give no details or items, for I keep no accounts, and never have. But, speaking in the gross, I believe it cost somewhat less than thirty shillings a head a day. Doubtless, it may be done for less. The best rule in such matters, of course, is, if you can afford it, to have what you want, and what will make a pleasure pleasant. As to equipment, what you need actually carry along with you is so little, that the statement of it would appear to people at home ridiculous. But, then, you can send on by the Post from place to place not only your heavy luggage, but such articles as your hat, if you are youthful, or old-fashioned enough to take a hat with you, and your spare pair of walking boots, and every thing else you may wish to have occasionally.

And here I have a suggestion to throw out, which occurred to me while I was on the tramp. What put it into my head was the incongruity of hotel life with excursions amid such scenes. In the Rocky Mountains the great enjoyment of the year is camping out in the fine season. In Syria and in India people travel with their tents. Why should we not camp out, and travel with our tents, in July and August in Switzerland; and so break loose altogether from the hotels? One mule, or horse, would carry the tent and all the tent furniture. If sometimes, but such a necessity would seldom arise, you had to pitch your tent on damp grass land, no inconvenience, I believe, would ensue. I have slept on a damp meadow under a tent on a bare plank, and was none the worse for it. And with the addition of a little hay, or straw, upon the plank, and upon that a waterproof sheet, you would have a luxurious bed for one who had walked five-and-twenty miles, and had not been under a roof during the day. The tent-mule might carry three light planks, each six feet long; for I will suppose that the party consists of two travellers, and a guide who also acts as muleteer. A saucepan, kettle, gridiron, and a few stores, to be renewed as required, would be necessary. Were the weather to prove unaccommodating there would always be the hotels at hand to take refuge in. A month of such campaigning would be very independent; and, I believe, very healthful and enjoyable.

At Sierre we took the rail for Aigle. There were a great many tedious delays on the way: one at almost every station. But to complain would be unreasonable, for, of course, the natives like to get as much as they can for the fares they have paid; and the lower the fare the greater the gain, if they get much of the rail for it. It was near 6 o'clock when we reached Aigle, where we intended to set up our head-quarters for some days, while looking out for a winter residence for my wife and the little man.

The night was still, and clear. In that unpolluted atmosphere, and among the mountains, the bright, soft, gleaming of the moon—it was now a little beyond the full—as it brings out the silvered peaks, and seems to darken the ravines, casts, as old Homer [*] noted

---

[*] As when in heaven the stars
Are shining round about the lustrous moon,
Exceeding bright; and all the air is still;
And every jutting peak, and beacon point
Stands clear, e'en to the wooded slopes below;
And the whole field of ether, opened out
Unfathomable, shows each particular star;

long ago, a pleasing spell over you; and you become indisposed to mar the silence of nature with a word. The spell, however, on this occasion was somewhat broken by the disturbing effect of continuous lightning, in the direction of the head of the valley, though the horizon was undimmed, throughout its whole circumference, by so much as a trace of haziness.

Of this witching power of the moon all people appear to be conscious. But how does it come to act upon us in this way? Many, doubtless, have tried to analyze, and get to the bottom of the feeling. I would suggest that the effect is produced by an unconscious comparison of the moon with the sun; and, then, by an unconscious inference drawn from

> And at the sight the shepherd to his heart
> Is fill'd with gladness.—ILIAD viii. 551.

I have essayed a rendering of this famous simile, not because I hope to succeed where so many are supposed to have failed, but because, as may be believed of a country parsonage, I have not a single translation of it at hand. It may be objected to the one I am driven to offer that the unfathomableness of the field of ether is a modern idea; and that Homer meant immensity in the direction, not of the profundity of the celestial space, but in the direction of its expansion. Our idea, however, embraces the whole of Homer's, and goes beyond it.

The double mention of the stars is hardly tautological; for the first mention of them is an indispensable stroke in the sketch, which was intended to convey to our minds the idea of a fine bright night; while the shining of so many particular stars in the immeasurable field of heaven is the point of the simile. As many as are the stars visible in such a sky, so many were the camp fires of the Trojan bivouac on the broad plain.

the comparison. The sun is the lord of our waking hours, and, as respects the moon, is our standard of comparison. Whatever we think of we must think of in reference to something else, that something else being the leading and most familiar object of the class the thing, at the moment thought about, belongs to, except it be the leading object itself, when the reverse reference is made. When, then, we look at the moon, there is a reference in the mind to the ideas and feelings, the results of our experience, we have about the sun. We may not be aware of this, but it is so, and cannot be otherwise. The sun is what gives us our conception of a large luminous body, apparently moving, majestically, round our earth. Having, then, made this comparison unconsciously—if it were done consciously there would be no spell, or witchery—we note the differences. The light is not the same. It does not penetrate to the recesses of objects. It does not give clear definition. It does not enable us to make out surfaces at a distance. It is not dazzling. It does not enable the beholder to distinguish colours. There is something spectral about it. But, above all, it is light unaccompanied by warmth. The substratum of our thought, as we look at the moon, is the sun: yet everything is different. The inference, again unconsciously arrived at, is that of the wondrous variety, combined with unspeakable magnitude, and other deeply affecting particulars, in these the greatest works, as they strike us at the moment, of the dimly-apprehended mystery of the universe. These half-formed thoughts, and their corresponding emotions, are brought home, not so much by the sun, because we are too familiar with it, and the objects we compare it with unconsciously are of inferior grandeur, as they are by the moon, that is, by the contemplation of it on a bright clear night. The moon stands far above all natural objects, indeed, it stands almost alone, in possessing the means for producing, in the way I have supposed, on all minds the effect we are endeavouring to understand. And the effect is deepened by the character of the hour. It is night. All is still. There is nothing to distract attention; nothing to dissipate the effect.

It will help us here, if we see that it is, in part, the same reason, which impels the dog to bay the moon. With him, as with ourselves, the standard of comparison is the sun. The light of the full moon invites him to look out from his kennel. He sees, as he thinks, the sun in heaven. The sun has ever been to him the source of warmth as well as of light. He has come to connect the idea of light emanating from a great luminary in heaven with that of warmth. But this sun, he is looking at now, does not give him any warmth. It even appears to strike him with a chill. The light, too, which it emits has differences, which are very perceptible, but unwonted, and unintelligible.

It does not enable him to make out familiar objects in the way in which light ought. His nerves are affected by these differences and disappointments. His agitation increases. In the still night there is nothing to divert his thoughts. It becomes insupportable. He gives unconscious expression to his agitation. He bays the moon. It is an expression of deep distress.

These feelings of the dog may also in some respects be compared to the feelings that used to come over all mankind, and still come over the savage, and other untutored people, at the contemplation of an eclipse.

September 18.—The lightning of last night was not an empty threat, for this morning dense masses of cloud were rolling down the valley, and there was much rain. We had been talking of going up the *Dent du Midi*; but, as it was, we could not get out till late in the afternoon, and then it still continued to be showery. We managed, however, to see one of the factories for parquetry floors, of which there are several here. Their work is beautifully executed, and very cheap. It is sent all over the world. We saw some orders that had just been executed for Egypt, and for the United States.

The contrast between Aigle and Leukabad is complete. Here everything is new, and neat, and bright. Opposite to us, across the road—we were quite new ourselves—was a house, in its trim grounds, as new, and neat, and bright as freshly wrought stone, and fresh paint could make it. There was not a weather-stain upon it. At the bottom of our garden were a party of jabbering Italian masons running up what was to be a large *pension*. But the most conspicuous of the new things in Aigle was a grand hotel, a little way off, nearer the mountains: so new that the grounds were not yet laid out. And so it was with almost everything in this flourishing little place, which has secured its full share in the rapidly-growing prosperity of the country. Its attractions are that it has a dry soil; a warm, sunny situation; and cheerful views. The baths of Leukabad cannot keep it alive. The sunshine of Aigle gives it life. If the decay of Leukabad, and the prosperity of Aigle at all show that people now endeavour to retain health by natural means, whereas the plan formerly was to let it go, and then endeavour to recover it by very doubtful means, we may deem the world has, in this particular, grown somewhat wiser than it was of yore; and so far, to go back once more to our old friend, Homer, we may boast that we are better than our fathers.

CHAPTER XIII.

THE DRAMA OF THE MOUNTAINS

Non canimus surdis.—VIRGIL.

I WILL here give two or three pages to the blue boy. He is not at all aware that I am about to put him into print. The reader, I trust, will think that the betrayal of confidence involved in my doing so is not altogether unjustifiable. I mentioned that on the day we crossed the Grimsel, from the Rhone Glacier to Meiringen, he was unusually silent. He afterwards told me that he had then been engaged in composing a drama, which was to be entitled 'The Drama of the Mountains,' in which the most conspicuous mountains he had seen— he had in 1870 made the acquaintance of M. Blanc— were to be the *Dramatis Personæ*. Nothing more was said on the subject then, or afterwards. We have infantine productions of Dr. Johnson, Pope, the late Professor Conington, and of others. I now offer the following drama, as an addition to this kind of litera- ture. I can vouch for its entire authenticity and genuineness. It shall be printed from the blue boy's own MS. The whole composition was arranged in his mind, some days before it was put upon paper, without a hint or suggestion from anybody, and subsequently not a word was corrected, nor even a point in the stopping altered. It could not have been more entirely his own had he been the only soul in Switzerland at the time it was composed. He was alone, too, at the time it was put upon paper. On the first day we were at Aigle—I have just mentioned that it was a wet day—I found him writing it *currente calamo*; and on hearing what he was about, I immediately left the room.

I must premise that last summer I had read to him Shakespeare's Julius Cæsar (he was then translating Cæsar's Commentaries), and the Midsummer Night's Dream. On each of which occasions he immediately afterwards produced a drama of his own; one in the high classical style founded on Roman history, the other in the style of Bottom's interlude. His having had those two plays read to him is the extent of his acquaintance with dramatic literature.

Those who may happen to have no personal acquaintance with his *dramatis personæ*, will allow a word or two on the appropriateness of the parts imagined for them. Blanc, of course, is Emperor in his own, the old, right: from his shoulders and upwards he is higher than any of his people. So with

Rosa: she has the same fitness for being Empress. Weishorn and Jungfrau are, beyond controversy, worthy of being, as the order of nature has made them, Prince and Princess Imperial. Cervin (the blue boy thinks in French, and so he calls Matterhorn by his French name), by reason of his signal and conspicuous uprightness, is the best of Prime Ministers. Schreckhorn's name and character fit him for the Ministry of Police, and prepare us for his horrible treason. Simplon has conferred on him the place of the Emperor's Messenger, on account of his services to the world in supporting the most serviceable of the great passes into Italy. We are not surprised at finding Silberhorn acting as Chancellor of the Exchequer. Mönch appropriately counsels peace. Finsteraarhorn, it will be observed, is taunted with hardly daring to show his face: a sarcastic allusion to the difficulty there is of getting a view of this mountain.

That the Empire of the Mountains was transferred to the Potentate of the Himalaya, was intended not only as an illustration of the bad policy of calling in to our assistance one stronger than ourselves—the mistake the horse made when he entered into a league with man to drive the stag from the contested pasture—but, also, as an application, and this was the main idea, of the broad simple principle of *detur digniori*.

THE DRAMA OF THE MOUNTAINS.

Dramatis Personæ.

BLANC, *emperor of the Alps.*
ROSA, *his wife.*
CERVIN, *his prime-minister.*
JUNGFRAU, *his daughter.*
WEISHORN, *his son.*
FINSTERAARHORN, *Jungfrau's husband.*
MÖNCH, *the priest.*
SCHRECKHORN, *the police-agent.*
SIMPLON, *messenger of the Alps.*
SILBERHORN, *treasurer.*

CHIMOULARI, *king of the Himalaya.*
DWALAGIRI, *his prime-minister.*
EVEREST, *his son.*

Prologue.

The empire of the Alps consists of a large number of European mountains, who think themselves the highest in the world; but it is not so, for the kingdom of the Himalaya is still higher and wiser. In the empire of the Alps, there had been internal disturbances between Blanc, the emperor, and Schreckhorn, the police-agent, in which Schreckhorn had mostly had the advantage and had shut the others up in a prison. But they escaped and applied to Chimoulari, king of the Himalaya, to help them, which he accordingly did, and defeated Schreckhorn. Chimoulari then received the empire of the Alps, and was then emperor of all the mountains in the world.

ACT I.

Scene I.

Blanc's *Palace.*

(*Enter* Blanc, Cervin, Weishorn, Jungfrau, Rosa, Finsteraarhorn, Mönch.)

BLANC.

Are we all met?

WEISHORN.

Yes, we are; we must not speak too loud, for Schreckhorn is outside the door.

CERVIN.

Schreckhorn outside the door! impossible!

FINSTERAARHORN.

Fear nothing.

CERVIN.

Finster, really, this is too bad : you wish to have us all in the lockup; yes, you who hardly dare to show your face !

ROSA.

Blanc, my husband, please send Finster out.

JUNGFRAU.

Blanc, don't, don't.—Rosa, what do you mean ; do you wish to deliver Finster into the hands of Schreckhorn?

MÖNCH.

Peace ! peace ! (*Exeunt omnes.*)

(*Enter* Schreckhorn *and* Silberhorn.)

SCHRECKHORN.

Silberhorn, pay me your debts.

SILBERHORN.

Please, my lord.

SCHRECKHORN.

Please is nothing to me ; pay !

SILBERHORN.

Blanc, come and help me. (*Enter* BLANC.)

SCHRECKHORN.

I condemn you both to lose fifty feet of your height.

BLANC.

Ah ! (*Exeunt omnes*).

SCENE II.

The Same.

(*Enter* BLANC *and* SIMPLON.)

BLANC.

Would it not be better if you called in Chimoulari ?

SIMPLON.

Yes, I will immediately. (*Exeunt duo.*)

SCENE III.

The Same.

(*Enter* BLANC, CHIMOULARI, DWALAGIRI, *and* EVEREST.)

CHIMOULARI.

Blanc, what do you want ?

BLANC.

To make war against Schreckhorn.

DWALAGIRI.

That is very easy.

EVEREST.

I will be general. (*Exeunt.*)

Scene IV.

The Same.

(*Enter* SCHRECKHORN *and* EVEREST.)

EVEREST.

Down with Thee.

SCHRECKHORN.

I will bring thee to nothing!

(EVEREST *knocks down* SCHRECKHORN, *kills him, and goes out.*)

Scene V.

The Same.

(*Enter* BLANC, CHIMOULARI, *and* EVEREST.)

EVEREST.

I have killed Schreckhorn.

CHIMOULARI.

Now, Blanc, give me the Empire of the Alps.

BLANC.

Must I yield it? yes, I suppose.

(EVEREST *and* BLANC *exeunt.*)

CHIMOULARI.

Now am I monarch of all around me! let me rejoice.

I do not give this little drama as a wonderful work for a child of between nine and ten, but to show what I think any child of average powers might do, spontaneously and with pleasure, if only parents and teachers could be brought to understand that the area of their teaching should be expanded to its natural limits, that is to the history of man, and to a general acquaintance with our earth. The proper starting point for the former is the history, in its widest sense, of the towns and localities with which the child is familiar; and for the latter the natural objects, mountains, rivers, valleys, plains, vegetation, animal life, meteorology, &c., of the same localities. The teacher should then pass on, in both these departments, from what has been understood, because it has been seen, to what will be understood, though not seen, because it differs in certain particulars, that can be explained, from what is already understood. So much for the area: and an equally great change must be brought about in the manner of teaching. We must adopt the natural method as well as the natural area; that is to say, we must teach orally and conversationally. In this way only can what is taught to a child be made intelligible. And if it be not made intelligible it cannot possibly interest. One step more: all about man and nature, that has thus been taught orally and conversationally, should always be subsequently repeated in the child's own words. This, among many other great advantages, cultivates as nothing else can, because, again, in the natural way, both the power of attention and the power of continuous extemporary expression. Teaching by the book and by heart—well so phrased, for the understanding has nothing to do with it, and it takes all heart out of a child—has, among others, this conspicuous evil, that at the cost to the child of compulsory ignorance, and gratuitously-engendered aversion to mental effort, it saves nothing, except the necessity, in the teacher, of knowing anything about what he professes to teach.

CHAPTER XIV.

ON SWISS HOTELS

In this the antique, and well-noted face
Of plain old form is much disfigured.—SHAKESPEARE.

FOR the word or two I have to say about the Swiss monster hotels, I can make the one mentioned at the close of the twelfth chapter my *point de départ* with safety; for I never entered it, and only know from what I saw outside, that it is fire-new, and as monstrous as new. As you look at one of these modern caravansaries, you are amused at thinking how precisely everything in it is the facsimile of all that you have seen in a score of others. The Swiss believe, and act, too, on the belief, that they have reduced hotel-keeping to an exact science; among them, therefore, in this matter, there cannot be any longer two opinions about the form of, or the way of doing, any one thing whatsoever. Everywhere the building itself appears arranged, externally and internally, on the same plan. Of an hotel, as of a five-pound note, there can be but one idea. In either case any deviation from the archetypal paradigm would disqualify the thing produced from being regarded as that which it professes to be.

As to life within the hotel, everywhere you have the same breakfast: coffee, two kinds of bread (the more solid kind almost always sticky and sour, the flour having been made from imperfectly ripened and imperfectly harvested grain), butter that is somewhat insipid, and honey that will inevitably soil your fingers, and perhaps trouble your interior. Exact science has demonstrated, beyond controversy, that precisely this breakfast, for every day in the three hundred and sixty-five, hits with mathematical rigour the point at which the wants and rights of the traveller —though, indeed, he has no business himself to think about his having any rights or wants at all—meet the scientifically regarded economies of the innkeeper. This unvarying breakfast is everywhere served to you on the same unvarying china—always white, solid, and heavy. Exact science informs us that if china of this kind be used there is a smaller amount of breakage, and that replacements are easy: and from exact science there is no appeal. That you who have to use it would prefer a little variety now and then has nothing at all to do with the matter.

And then as to your dinner: it also is always the same. As the dinner-bell reminds you of this, you find that you are agitated by an involuntary shudder.

Always, and everywhere, the same viands cooked in the same fashion; and served, too, again on the same white, solid, heavy china. There is the inevitable *filet de bœuf*: more inevitable than the conscience of an evil deed, for that does not rise up before you throughout your whole life every day. One feels that one could almost give a year's income never to see or hear mention made of this *filet de bœuf* any more. Then come mutton and chicken, the latter always with salad. Sometimes, however, one of the two latter is replaced with veal. But the beef, the mutton, the veal, and the chicken, before they were roasted or ragouted, had been passed through the already-mentioned bath, in order to make the *potage* with which you commenced your repast. The mind, encouraged by the wilfulness of the palate, refuses to form a conception of a sirloin of beef, or of a leg of mutton, that had been boiled before it was roasted; or of a beef-steak, or of a mutton-chop, that had passed through the digester on its way to the gridiron; or of a veal-cutlet that has had its natural insipidity aggravated by this exhaustive treatment. The regale concludes with, every day, the same dried figs and the same raisins; or if it be late enough in the season, with the same plums and the same pears, so called, eked out by the same little cakes and the same little biscuits. Swiss hotel science repudiates entirely the ideas of roasted joints, and almost entirely of puddings. As to the wine, it has not, as might be expected, any exceptional merit; and as to the varieties indicated on the *carte*, they do not always correspond with the varieties of Nature: for science has demonstrated that a variety of labels constitute a variety of kinds.

You are pursued by this scientific sameness to your bed-room; and are soon haunted in your dreams with the idea that you are carrying about with you everywhere your bed and your bed-room furniture. As to the looking-glass, it is never on a dressing-table, but always nailed to the wall; for the science of Swiss hotel-keeping has discovered that the frame for a glass of this kind is cheaper than what would be required for one placed on a table; and that, besides, there is a far less chance of the glass itself being broken when it has become a fixture on the wall. This, however, obliges you to encumber yourself with a glass of your own; for a man cannot shave by a glass that has not its back to the light. Not even in the lock of your bed-room door is there a shadow of variation. It is always of iron, for iron is cheaper than brass; and always of the same form and size: they must all have been made at the same factory. And this unfailing black iron lock, always of the same size, is always attached to the surface of the door instead of being let into it. Your candlestick, too, is always the same —you fall back again on the theory of a single factory —a mere pedestal of brass with a glass cup at the top—I have, however, occasionally seen them without this glass cup—to receive the overflowings of the compo, which is often euphoniously described in the bill as *bougie*. But possibly where the glass is now wanting, it may, as exact science does not recognise disturbing causes, have originally existed. The candle again, in the unvarying candlestick, is always everywhere the same, with a wick that is but little more than a thread. The *rationale* of this tenuity of the wick is that the compo may not be consumed too rapidly for science. But then the least gust of air, or a careless quick movement of the candle, extinguishes it. You then have to relight it with a sulphurous lucifer, always everywhere sulphurous.

As to the traveller himself, he soon comes to find that he is not regarded as a thinking, feeling, and acting, or in any way independent entity. He is not supposed to have any likes or dislikes; any wants or ways of his own: he is merely one of the constituent molecules of an aggregated mass of inert, insentient matter, which must be manipulated in a certain fixed manner, which the discoveries of hotel science have shown to be necessary in order to produce a certain determinate result in the form of a certain amount of profit. Or he may compare himself to one of the milch-cows belonging to the hotel, which must have that amount of attention bestowed upon it, that amount of daily provender, and of that kind, and at night that berth and bedding, which at the least cost will produce the greatest amount of milk. Finding yourself treated in this way, merely as a unit in a large herd, you become aware that you are losing your sense of personal identity. How can you go on believing that you are what Nature made you, or that you have any special nature at all of your own, when, from being constantly herded with a hundred other people, all fed during the day, and provided for during the night, in precisely the same fashion, everything is conspiring to impress upon you the self-obliterating conviction that you are exactly what all the rest are: nothing more, nothing less, and nothing different?

Of your associate molecules, your fellow milch-cows, in these monster hotels, the majority speak your own language. Of these perhaps you will regard with most sympathy and favour the mountain-climbers, although you may yourself have ceased, as will probably be the case, if you are on the shady side of fifty, to look upon athletics, pure and simple, as the object of life. Still these vigorous specimens of youthful British humanity have set themselves something to do, and are doing it; and it is something that requires, at all events, enterprise and endurance. Not many of them, however, are to be found in the most aggravated form of the monster hotel, for that belongs to the towns rather than to the mountains. Another class is composed of those who do not climb, but are merely enthusiasts on the subject of mountain scenery. Of these the most gushing are of the fairer sex. With them, too, you can go as far as they go; though not quite to the extent of applying the epithet of 'lovely' to everything indiscriminately, even to rugged peaks, and rivers of ice; nor of being consumed by their uncontrollable desire to know, for a few moments, the name of every peak and point that happens to be in sight, and to arrive at this evanescent knowledge by the process of questioning the bystanders. You meet also multitudes of lawyers, clergymen, schoolmasters, and literary men. These, speaking generally, are the *élite* of the corresponding classes you have at home. Another large item is made up of men engaged in trade and business, from London and the manufacturing districts. It is a very good thing for them that they are able to leave their counters, and counting-houses, and factories; and to exchange, for a time, the murky atmosphere, and the moil and toil of the routine of their ordinary lives for the mountains. This makes you glad to see them also.

Everybody knows that our Transatlantic cousins will be met with everywhere in shoals, and nowhere are these shoals greater than in Switzerland. Some of those you fall in with will be New York shoddy-lords, some will be Pennsylvanians who have struck oil, some will be successful speculators in real estate in the neighbourhood of rising western cities. But if you have known the American in his own country, and in his own home, and are not dissatisfied with a man, merely because he cannot pronounce the Shibboleths of Eton and Oxford, you will be glad to make the acquaintance of a large proportion of the Americans you encounter. They are clear-headed and hard-headed; men who hold their own ground, and are, at the same time, sociable and friendly.

The Germans come next in number to those who speak our own tongue, they are quiet, honest, and earnest; and have evidently come to Switzerland for the purpose—there is no doubt about that—of constructing in their minds a correct idea of the nucleus, and central watershed, of Europe. But, as few of us speak German, there is little intercourse between them and English travellers.

Among the inmates of all these large hotels, because it is in them that such wanderers find most nearly what suits them, there remains a conspicuous *residuum*, that of those who have nothing in the world to do, and who, as thoroughly as if they were peak-and-pass-men, do it. They belong to all countries: Russia, France, England, and America supply each its respective quota. They are, for the most part, carefully, sometimes rather loudly got up: they have not much else to attend to. And from this, perhaps also from a little assumption in their manner, they contrive somewhat to obtrude themselves on the general notice of the world in the hotel. They belong to the class of failures, the *coups manqués*, of civilised humanity. They are the waifs and strays of modern society, with money enough, and often plenty of it, to live out of their own country. Sometimes with not enough left to live at home as they once did. They have no sense of home, nor love of country; but a sufficient sense of the duty men owe to themselves. You sometimes hear them intimating, as a reason for their voluntary expatriation, that they do not quite like their own country, and countrymen—perhaps no great proof of the demerit of either, or of their own judgment. The largest portion of the self-depreciators of this kind belong to the English quota of the class.

The disciples of so exalted and serene a philosophy, having got beyond home, and country, and all inconveniently large ideas of duty, can have no prejudices. Pet ideas, however, like the rest of the world, they have; and the one they most pet is expressed in our time-honoured, home-manufactured phrase, though amongst ourselves its use is prompted by the anxieties and fears of deep love, that 'the sun of England has set.' This is quite intelligible in a certain class of Frenchmen and Russians. The wish, with them, was father to the thought. They, as might have been expected, have become dazzled at the excess of light which radiates from our sun, and can now only look at it through the green lens. This old familiar phrase, coming from such oracular lips (but the announcement as it comes from them is history, not prophecy, for it is the announcement of a *fait accompli*), is accepted, with thorough satisfaction, by those of our countrymen who are disposed to regard its promulgators with submissive admiration, and are vainly endeavouring to form themselves on their model. They are only too thankful for any crumbs which fall from such tables. But be this as it may, the business of these wanderers is to go up and down, and to and fro, upon the earth. In this respect their occupation resembles the description the reprobate sprite gave of his. And he, too, had lost the sense, if we may so put it, of home, and country, and duty ; and must also have had in his eyes some tint of green. But they go only where locomotion and life are easy ; and where they may expect to find the society of congenial sprites, who will not ruffle them, will not be blind to their merits, and will take them, occasionally, at the price they set upon themselves.

It may, then, be placed on the credit side of the account of these scientifically managed hotels, though, at the time, one, being averse to entering them, and not averse to leaving them, is not disposed to credit them with much good, that they supply some materials for 'the proper study of mankind.' It was not, however, for the purpose of obtaining facilities for the prosecution of this study that you came to Switzerland: perhaps, rather it was that you might lose sight of it for a time.

CHAPTER XV.

BERNE—SWISS FOUNTAINS — ZURICH — MUSEUM OF RELICS FROM ANCIENT LAKE-VILLAGES—BAUR EN VILLE—RÉCOLTE DES VOYAGEURS—C'EST UN PAUVRE PAYS

> Beyond compare, of all things best
> Is water.—PINDAR.

September 19.—We spent the day at Vevey. Vineyards were everywhere along the sides of the railway. It is pleasing to note the care with which the vine, that peerless gift of Nature's bounty to man, is cultivated; how the land is terraced and fenced, and how scrupulously clean it is kept. This indicates the value of the land that is adapted to its growth, and is in keeping with the character of the gift. Had a swim in the lake. My first plunge into it was thirty-one years ago, on returning to Geneva from a walking expedition to Chamouni.

On the following day (dates are no longer needed, for our excursion was now ended, and I was returning home, on my own hook) I started for Zurich by way of Berne. The country, as seen from the rails, looks as if it were fertile, and carefully cultivated. The three points in which, to the eye of a passer-by, their agriculture appears to differ most from ours are, first, the greater cleanness of the land. I know no farmers —of course there are many exceptions, and notably where there is steam-ploughing — who cultivate so many weeds as the famous British farmer. Secondly, their not giving to their land so much manure as we do. One, however, may be mistaken on this point. And, thirdly, in the absence of live stock from the fields. I understood that the price of land is very high : the figures given to me were higher than the price of equally good agricultural land would come to here at home.

Since I was last at Berne, it appeared to me that a great deal had been done in the way of extension and improvement. The place has the look of having thriven much, and of still continuing to thrive. A few years ago a neighbouring stream was diverted, and made to flow through the heart of the city. It supplies, in its new course, several copious public fountains. These are sculptured and decorated, as if the people loved the water, and wished to heighten their pleasure at seeing, and welcoming, and using it. One of the most pleasing sights in a Swiss town—it is the same down to the smallest village — is this abundance of good water with which it is supplied. It is ever in sight, for every use of man and beast. In our English cities there was no want—the omission is still far from having been set right—that was so conspicuously neglected. And this, though an abundant supply of good water is not only a first necessity of life, but equally so of civilisation. The reasons of our negligence, in a matter of so much importance, are not far to seek. As the Swiss manage their own affairs, their first care is to provide themselves with what all need; and, evidently, the first thing of this kind to be attended to is the water-supply. Their system, too, of political, and, as respects the land, to some extent, of possessive equality, has engendered a sentiment of philanthropy; not of the charitable, or condescending, kind, but a general desire in all to attend to the rights, the wants, and the well-being of all. It would be distressing to all alike to find that any one had not as much water as he could require, supplied to him in the handiest way, in which it might be possible for the opportunities, and combined resources of the community to effect this.

Different influences have been at work amongst ourselves. The community has not managed its own affairs in such a manner, and on such a footing, as that the wants and interests of the humbler, and more helpless, classes should be as much felt, and attended to, as the wants and interests of the well-to-do classes, and of those who are able to take care of themselves. This has hindered the importance, or rather the necessity, of an abundant supply of water presenting itself, generally, to men's intelligence, and conscience, as really one of the primal cares of the community. This has not been one of the points which town councils, and rate-payers (perhaps because they were rate-payers) have seen in a proper light. There has been something which has stood in the way of their seeing it at all. Then there have been influential bodies in every community, whose interests lay in an opposite direction. I mean the water companies, and the manufacturers, and retailers of intoxicating liquors. You could hardly expect them to have seen very distinctly that it was the duty, and the interest, of the community to provide everywhere, and for everybody, a visible, constant, gratuitous supply of fresh, running, sparkling water. Nor, indeed, could the government of the country be expected to be more sharp-sighted in this matter than the local administrations; for it had to collect an enormous revenue for the purpose of enabling it to pay the interest of an enormous debt. There was, therefore, something to indispose it, also, to supply a want, the supply of which must inevitably reduce the number of millions it was collecting, every year, on the production and consumption of intoxicating drinks. These are the reasons which have issued in the fact, that water has been kept out of, or not brought into, the sight of the inhabitants of our English towns, and villages. It was not because water could be supplied on easier terms in Switzerland than in this country, because we find as much attention paid to its abundant free supply in some other continental countries, for instance in Italy, as in Switzerland.

Everyone who will give the subject a little thought will come to the conclusion, that it is this neglect which is mainly answerable for some of the preventible maladies, and for much of the drunkenness, and so of the misery and crime, which afflicts our working classes. The efforts that have been made of late years to set up drinking-fountains in London, and in many of our towns, is an indication that in this supreme matter our eyes are beginning to be opened. When they are completely opened, a public, free, inexhaustible supply of the purest possible water will be the first care of every community, great and small; and drinking-fountains will, everywhere, offer an alternative to the gin-palace and public-house, and in winter as well as in summer.

To the reflecting mind, the overflowing sparkling fountains of the Swiss towns are very pleasing objects. So, too, to the natural eye, and ear, are the brawling stream in every valley, and the trickling rills on every hill-side. There is water, water, everywhere; and every drop to drink. This the pedestrian, at all events, will appreciate; and when the sun is bright, he will be thankful for it a dozen times a day.

At Zurich I was much interested by the public collection of objects, found at the bottom of the lake, and on the site of the old lake-villages. Herodotus mentions a powerful Thracian people, who dwelt in a similarly constructed city on Lake Prasias. The Irish and Scotch cranoges are also instances of ancient structures of the same kind. To this day, in New Guinea and Borneo, and in Africa, we find water-towns still inhabited. In all these cases it was the same necessity, that of providing against sudden attacks from more powerful neighbours, that suggested the idea. And if we may refer to the same class, the lagoon-protected infancy of Venice, then the Queen of the Adriatic, with her St. Mark's, and her palaces, owes her existence to the idea, from which originated, in a very old past, the little wooden huts of the Lake of Zurich.

The objects which have been recovered reveal the habits, arts, conditions of life, and much of the internal history of those who formed, and used them. About the events of their external history, though much of this can be pretty well imagined, of course they are silent. Nor have they anything to tell us in reply to the questions of who the people were, whence they came, or what became of them? The information they give us begins with the time when men, in central Europe, had not attained to a knowledge of metals, and were using implements of bone and stone for war, hunting, and domestic purposes. Abundance of their stone tools have been found, and also of specimens of the work done with them. For instance, some of the series of piles, upon which the dwellings were placed, and these piles are found by the hundred, we see were hacked to the point, which was to fit them for driving, with stone chisels and hatchets. And then, in other series of piles, we pass on to the era when stone had been superseded by bronze and iron tools. It is very interesting to have thus before us the actual tools, and the actual work done with them, together with ocular demonstration of the way in which, by the superiority of their work, the first metal tools superseded their perfected predecessors of stone.

Everything, one may almost say, has been preserved, and, too, in a most wonderfully perfect state. Besides the tools and weapons in great variety, there are their nets and clothes, their pottery in jars and cups, and utensils for many purposes, the bones of the animals on which they feasted, the different kinds of fruit they had gathered from the forest, and of grain they had cultivated. In all these matters the old lake-dwellers have bequeathed to us the means of comparing notes with them. The bones that have been found of the ox, the sheep, and the dog show that the varieties of the respective species then kept by the dwellers in this neighbourhood were not precisely identical with any of their varieties now known. They were, too, great hunters, and game was abundant in the locality. Among the vast quantities of bones of wild animals, that have been found, are those of the wolf, the bear, the beaver, the wild boar, the stag, the European bison (which still exists in the Forest of Lithuania, and is the largest quadruped next after the rhinoceros), and of the urus, the aboriginal wild ox of Europe, which is now extinct.

They were also agriculturists. One of the kinds of wheat they cultivated was what we call the Egyptian, or Mummy Wheat. Some of the specimens of this could not be more perfect had they been only just harvested. It had several small ears ranged round a main central ear, and from this reason sometimes goes by the name of the hen-and-chickens wheat. It is interesting to know that so distinctly marked a variety was being cultivated at so remote a period, on the banks of the Lake of Zurich, by these trans-Alpine barbarians, and on the banks of the Nile, by the subjects of the early Pharaohs, at the same time. Here is a kind of possible connection between the builders of Karnac and the builders of these pile-supported huts; and also a point in the history of one of our Cereals, of the birth, parentage, and education of all of which so little is known. Two kinds of millet, and a six-rowed variety of barley have also been found. These rude contributories to the ancestry of the modern European were at the same time collecting for food, from the neighbouring forests, sloes, bullaces, wild cherries, beech-mast, crab-apples, elder-berries, the hips of the wild rose, raspberries, blackberries, and hazel-nuts; for well-preserved remains of all these have been found on the sites of the lake-villages. Some of the specimens are supposed to show slight differences from the same fruits now growing wild in the neighbourhood. These differences, if they do really exist, must, notwithstanding their slightness, indicate a long lapse of time.

They also cultivated flax. Nets and lines made from it, together with the very scales of the fish the nets and lines caught, and the woven cloth, with the very fringes that decorated the dresses into which it had been formed, and even the weights used in working the looms, are all here, to teach us how widely spread, in very early times, were the most necessary of the useful arts. There has, then, been no solution in the continuity of man's history. His wants were from the first substantially the same as they are at this day; and these wants were from the first supplied by the same contrivances as at this day, with the difference that, in every age, the contrivances were raised to the level of the knowledge, and consequent resources, of the times. The spinning-jenny, and the power-loom, in a few large cities, are now doing for millions what the wives and daughters of these old lake-dwellers, seated in summer on the wooden platform above the water, and in winter within the hut, did for each separate family. The wants of what appear to us as the primæval times, but which were in fact very far from that, have been enlarged and multiplied, in proportion as man's means for meeting them became improved and enlarged; and this kind of growth in the old wants, consequent upon growth in our means for supplying them, constitutes what is generally meant by progress. And this material progress it is, which makes possible moral and intellectual progress, the glory, and privilege, and happiness of man.

One cannot help comparing these relics of the old lake-village with the copiously furnished stateliness of its modern neighbour, the city of Zurich. You set them, in thought, by the side of its handsome streets of stone houses, its rich shops, its large factories, especially of iron, in which labour is so skilfully organised, and so scientifically directed, its university, its general intelligence, its conscious efforts to cultivate, and turn to account, that intelligence, its accumulated wealth, its patriotism, its knowledge of, and connection with, every part of the world. But varied, complex, great, and interesting as all this is, still it is only the step now at length reached, by the labour of many generations, in the true and natural development of what was existing on the lake some thousands of years ago. Society, such as it was, in those old days, in the rude, wood-built, water-protected huts was the embryo of society, such as it now is in the proud, modern city. How natural, then, is the jealous care with which it guards these old relics; for if they do not speak to the Zurichers of their own actual ancestors they show them what were the germs out of which has grown their present condition.

I spoke of the large Swiss hotels exactly as they impressed me. I found in them nothing that was attractive to me. Why it was so I endeavoured to explain. I must, however, here note that what I then said is not applicable to Baur's Hotel at Zurich. I said as much to the manager on leaving, though I was sure that he must often have received similar commendation from others. The house is as well ordered as you would wish to see your own home. The bedrooms are of a good size, and well furnished. The table is liberal. The *cuisine* good. A wholesome Rhenish wine is supplied at dinner. The attendants are clean and attentive. Everything you are likely to want is provided; nor are there any traps set, or any wish apparent that you should call, for extras. For meals at irregular hours there is an excellent *restaurant* in the house, distinct from the dining *salon*.

This hotel, though large, has none of the cold, hard, obtrusive air of its monster brethren. In short, things are so managed that you feel that you are in a good, comfortable hotel, and not in a large factory, where bales of travellers, yourself a bale, are undergoing the process, like truck-loads of brute material, of scientific manipulation. I was at Baur *en ville*. Baur *au lac*, at a distance of three or four minutes' walk, is, I suppose, managed in the same fashion, and is the same kind of thing.

But how about the *note*? I suppose wages, and the price of provisions, must be much the same in Zurich as in other Swiss towns, but the *note* did not lighten my purse as much as experience would have led me to have expected. A man, then, even an innkeeper, may sometimes be found, whose merits are obvious to the world, but who enhances them—and this is true virtue—by himself setting a low price upon them.

Hitherto the risings and settings of the sun had been, as I mentioned, almost achromatic. I suppose on account of the clearness of the atmosphere. But now a great change had taken place; there had been falls of rain, and even of snow, and the air had become full of moisture, and there was much cloud; in consequence, there were in the evenings some most glorious atmospheric fields of colour. I keep in mind one of these sunsets above the rest, because of the way in which it placed the murky, swart outline of the ridges and peaks of the Jura in contrast with the usual oranges and reds above, but which, though seen so often, one never tires of looking at. It is almost enough to condemn a country house, that the sunset cannot be seen from it.

I have another reason for recollecting this sunset. I was with several persons at the moment who were observing it together. Among these were two Swiss gentlemen. But in the change of weather which it indicated, they only saw a hint that this year's *récolte des voyageurs*, as they phrased it, was drawing to a close: a true harvest, which costs Switzerland little, and is got in with not unthrifty husbandry, and which one is glad should benefit so many, both among those who do the harvesting, and among those who are harvested. A French gentleman, however, who happened to be present, and had been spending the summer on the banks of the Lake of Geneva—it might be inferred that his recollections of the way in which he had himself been harvested, were not in all respects pleasant—turned to me with the aside, *C'est un pauvre pays.*

CHAPTER XVI.

A REMARK ON SWISS EDUCATION

The proper study of mankind is man.—POPE.

IT has long been my practice, wherever I find myself, to inquire into the provisions made for education, and into the modes of teaching adopted; and, also, by observation, and talking to the people themselves, to do what I can, as far as opportunities go, to collect materials for enabling me to form an opinion on the results and fruits of what has been done. I did this wherever I was on this excursion; and as it was my object in going to Zurich to see its Polytechnic University, I will here give one of the conclusions I came to on the subject of Swiss education.

It was constructed by the Swiss to suit their own wants. That it does admirably well. Such a system, however, would be very far from suiting equally well that large class amongst ourselves, who are destined for either a public life, or for what may be called the semi-public life of our men of property, and of a large proportion of those whose special work is that of one of the learned professions: at all events, both law and divinity, as practised in this country, have direct connections with political life. The Swiss, however, are a small, and a poor people, whose affairs are, in the main, managed locally. They have no need of trained statesmen; they have no *haute politique.* Speaking generally, they are a nation of peasant-proprietors, artizans, manufacturers, and tradesmen. At present, in many parts of the country, the only tritons among the minnows are the innkeepers. Manufactures, which mean also commerce, are, here and there, introducing a moneyed class; and the hundreds of thousands of pounds, spent every year in the country, by tens of thousands of travellers, are enriching bankers, and, through many channels, many others. Now the education such a people requires is one that will make intelligent artizans, intelligent manufacturers, and intelligent tradesmen; and which will give to that portion of the population for whom work cannot be found at home, sufficient intelligence to dispose them to go into foreign countries; and will enable them, when there, to take their bread out of the mouths of the inhabitants of those countries. This is what the Swiss system aims at doing. And wherever it is well carried out,—of course this is done much better in the Protestant than in the Catholic cantons,—it attains its aim. In many of the Catholic cantons the people are content to be as their fathers were: they do not see very distinctly the advantage of cultivating the intelligence of their children; and it cannot be supposed that the village priest will be very forward in enlightening them on this point.

What the Swiss system, true to its object, sets itself to teach is the languages that will be useful in business, arithmetic, mathematics, the principles of the useful arts, and the elements of the sciences. All this is just what will enable the Swiss to get on in the careers that will be open to them. They are an intensely practical people; and these thoroughly practical subjects they take care shall be taught sufficiently for the purpose they have in view. They have no idea of not getting their pennyworth for their penny. Their philanthropy, and their love of home, the unfailing and fruitful source of so many virtues, make them desirous of giving every chance to their children; and they are interested in, and proud of, and spend their money on, their schools for their children's sake. All this is just as it should be. It is a very good thing for them; and, as far as it goes, it would be a very good thing for us, if we had the same system at work here. It is exactly what is wanted for nine-tenths of our population; and what they must have if we are to keep our place in the world. But when this shall have been done, if there is ever to be a time when it will have been done, there will still remain one-tenth of our population, a number equal to, or greater than, that of the whole Swiss nation, which will be capable of receiving, and will need for the life that will be before them, something different from, and higher than, a Swiss education.

The Swiss system is large and liberal for a tradesman; it almost makes of him a gentleman. But for an English gentleman it would be narrow and illiberal. It would not properly qualify him for the careers that are open to him, and for the life that is before him. It is not the kind of culture that will produce statesmen, jurists, divines, orators, poets, historians, literary lay teachers, or philosophers. If, by the grace of nature, an English boy had been intended for any one of these vocations, to bring him up in the Swiss fashion would be to rob him of his birthright: and the more thoroughly the system had been applied to him, the more complete would be the robbery, and the greater the injustice and the injury.

An English gentleman has not been properly qualified for what is his work in life, unless his education has been such as to make him acquainted with the history of man, and with what may be called the sciences of humanity. By the sciences of humanity I mean ethics, economics, polity, jurisprudence, the history of opinion, the history of literature, dialectics, oratory. An acquaintance with these is what, from the first, should be kept in view. They should be worked up to from the beginning of the process, for they are the crown and completion of the mental training he will require. They are that training. And this is just what our system, not from intelligent and deliberate design, but from a happy accident, does in some degree attempt. It provides for it in the study of the history of Greece and Rome, two of the most important and instructive developments of the history of man; and, furthermore, in the direct study of some of the above-mentioned sciences. I say it does this not so much by intelligent design, as by a happy accident, because that it is doing it at this day is merely the result of our having retained the classical system our forefathers established at a time when there was nothing else to teach; and which they established just because there was nothing else to teach then. We may now, knowing what we want, and what materials we have to work with, very much enlarge and improve their system. We may advance from the classics to general history and humanity; of course still retaining the classics, which contain the most important chapters in the history of the fortunes, of the culture, and of the mind of man. And this, which is just what we ought to do, is what, perhaps, we shall do, when we come to understand what it is that gives it its value, and makes it indispensable for us.

Another capital defect in a system, such as that of the Swiss, is that it does not cultivate, but rather represses and deadens, the imagination. This is the instrument of the creative faculty in man, that in which we make the nearest approach to, and which gives to man in the form and degree possible for him, the plastic power that is exhibited to us in the richness, and diversity, of nature. It is this which makes a man myriad-minded ; which enables him to look at things from all sides, and to see them in all lights; to regard them as minds most unlike his own regard them ; to be in his single self all men to all things ; it is what gives insight ; and the power of forming accurate and distinct conceptions of things in the three forms of what they actually are, of what they have been, and of what, with reference to other conceptions that have a bearing upon them, they ought to be. A man cannot be a poet, an orator, an artist, hardly an inventor, or discoverer, an historian, or a statesman, without the exercise of this faculty. His rank in any one of these fields of intellectual work will depend on the degree to which it has been developed within him ; and the kind of discipline it is under. Our system, in a rough, and haphazard, kind of a way, and again more by accident than by intelligent, deliberate design, does something for its cultivation, by the study of the poets and orators of Greece and Rome ; and by attempts at poetical composition. This is good as far as it goes ; but insufficient for the great purpose. And this insufficiency of the means we are employing is aggravated, when they have to be applied under the direction of masters and tutors, who possibly, and probably, too, have never given a thought to the nature and purposes of the imaginative faculty; and, therefore, are, of course, equally heedless of the right methods of using the means, that happen to be in their hands, for awakening, cultivating, and strengthening it.

Its proper cultivation in these times should not be confined to the poetry of the old world. That is valuable, not merely on account of its perfectness of form, but because it is one-sided, unchristian, and narrow. It is the poetry of a small, highly privileged class, when that small class was everything, and the bulk of mankind nothing. It is not the poetry of humanity broadly. The recognition of the humanity of all men equally constitutes one essential difference between the modern and the old world. And this limited, and somewhat abnormal, humanity of the ancient poetry is, furthermore, somewhat unconnected with a knowledge of, and love for, nature—the *milieu* of man. All this makes it very valuable as a study of a distinct development, under peculiar circumstances, of the poetic faculty. But it is insufficient. It is no substitute for an acquaintance with the poetry of the modern world; which, too, it should follow, and not precede. That is the truer and more normal development. It has additional roots, a wider range, a larger inspiration; it takes cognizance of what is in man, irrespective of conditions, or rather under every condition: and it also consciously regards man and nature connectedly; man's internal nature, and nature external to man, are to its apprehension correlated. Here, too, it has received a new revelation.

And the attempt to turn a child's mind in the direction of nature, and to give him some general acquaintance with nature, and with modern poetry, would be invaluable for another reason: for not only is this now necessary, as an indispensable part of mental culture for all, being a part of the rightful mental inheritance of those whose lot is cast in these times, but because experience has taught us that there are many minds, which have no aptitude for the acquisition of languages, either from some congenital defects, or, as is most probable, from some faults and omissions of early teaching and associations — but whatever may have been in their cases the cause is a matter of no consequence now: the mischief exists, and cannot be removed. Still, though deficient to this extent, they may have no disinclination for the study of nature: that, in the young, can hardly be possible. Here, then, is something that will enable them to live a not unworthy intellectual life. It is necessary for all: as a part of complete culture for those who are capable of complete culture; and, for those who are not, as a sufficient culture.

The advocates of the continuance—to the extent

and for the purposes I have indicated—of classical study will labour under a great and unfair disadvantage, as long as the classics shall be taught with but slight perception, on the part of those who teach them, of their bearing on the higher work of the day. As long as the main object of our public schools shall continue to be professedly linguistic, and that, too, in a somewhat narrow, and shallow fashion; and their tone, sometimes a little ostentatiously, at variance with that of the world, and of the day, for the work of which they ought to be a preparation (it was so with them originally) so long will the advocacy of classical studies be unfairly weighted with a sense of the justice of the charge of unreality brought against them, as now conducted. Whereas in the advocates of modern knowledge as the object and instrument of education, and in its teachers, there is none of this unreality, or want of connexion with the thought, and with the work, of the world that is stirring around us. We, however, hold that it is a different department of work and thought, to which the latter training mainly and primarily applies. A public man need not, as a public man, know anything of astronomy and geology; though, of course, he is behind the age, and his culture is incomplete, if he does not. Of all such subjects he ought, as an educated man, to have a general knowledge; and he will also be the better, as a public man, for having it; but what is primarily and indispensably required of him is a knowledge of man, and of all kinds of social phenomena in their whole range; what they are, how they came to be what they are, and how they affect man. Here his knowledge should be full and precise: and a very valuable part of this knowledge is contained in the literature of the old world. He ought to have lived through those ages. To have done so is a vast extension of experience of the most useful kind. But he cannot have lived through those times, unless he is familiar with the feelings and thoughts, and actions of the men of those times, together with the circumstances, and conditions, under which they so thought, and felt, and acted. And he cannot have this familiarity unless he has a knowledge of the very words, in which they, themselves, expressed, and described, those feelings, thoughts, and actions.

One word more. There is no knowledge so valuable as that of what is knowledge; nor any intellectual habit so valuable as that which disposes us in every thing to require knowledge, and to separate that which is knowledge from that which is not. Theoretically, there is no reason why either the study of language, or theology, should not be made a training for this knowledge, and for this habit. But as this is a matter of practice, as well as of theory, we must look at things as they are, and see where what we want is actually found, and what has in those cases produced it; and where there has been a failure in producing it, and what has been in those cases the cause of this failure. Who, then, are most conspicuous for knowing in what knowledge consists, and for the habit of requiring knowledge as a ground for thought and action, and for being ever on the alert to separate knowledge from its counterfeits? No one, I think, would hesitate in replying, those who have had some scientific training. And it is easy to see how scientific training gives this knowledge, and this habit. It makes no difference what the matter of the study be, whether the stars, or the fungi; whether the physiology of man, or of an earth-worm. The object is soon seen to be truth; and the motive is soon felt to be the satisfaction which truth gives to the mind, and the desire to escape, in the practical order, from the wastefulness, and the mischief of error. Whatever, therefore, is necessary for the attainment of truth is submitted to, or acquired, or eliminated, or avoided, in accordance with the exigency of each case. In these pursuits men learn to guard against appearances that they may not be misled by them; to sift evidence; to distinguish facts from supposed, or alleged, facts; to observe patiently and closely; to suspend judgment; to distinguish probability from certainty; to distinguish different degrees of probability; to distinguish what they know from what they wish; not to wish for anything but ascertained and demonstrable truth; to examine everything, and to hold fast only that which is demonstrably true; to guard against ambiguities in words; to use words for photographing facts, and not to make them a mist which obscures both the object of inquiry, and the paths which lead to it. As a matter of observation, and of fact, these are the habits of mind, which the scientific study of any subject inculcates, and makes natural to a man. They become his second nature. Of course they ought to be the nature of all educated people. And when a man's mind has been thus trained in the study, scientifically pursued, of any one subject, he applies these habits to the consideration of all other subjects, with which he may have to do: to those, with which he is not familiar, he addresses himself with the same ideas, and the same ways of thinking, as he does to that, with which he is familiar. He knows what knowledge is; and, while he can suspend his judgment, he cannot be satisfied with anything but knowledge. What he does not know upon these subjects he knows that he does not know. The study of language, and theology, if scientifically taught, are doubtless capable of supplying this training, but looking at our educated classes generally, and at those who have had administered to them the greatest amount of these two studies, it does not appear that the desired effect has been produced. If, then, these things are so, here is both something that should be an object, and something that is a defect, as things now are, in our higher education.

CHAPTER XVII.

ELSASS — LOTHRINGEN — METZ—GRAVELOTTE—MOTHER OF THE CURÉ OF STE. MARIE AUX CHÊNES—WATERLOO.

*It is a just award
That they who take, should perish by, the sword.*

I INCLUDED Mulhouse, Colmar, Strasbourg, Bitche, and Metz in my homeward journey. As I passed along, the higher peaks of the Vosges were white with recently fallen snow. It is not, however, the forest-clad mountains, and their snow-capped summits which interest most the thought of the traveller, as he traverses this district, now, but the consequences of that recent transference of power, of which the names just written down remind him: the cotton industry of Mulhouse and Colmar; the astonishing agricultural wealth of the neighbourhood of Strasbourg, where the land yields, side by side, in singular luxuriance the five agricultural products, sugar-beet, hops, wine, tobacco, and maize, which in Europe pay the best; the strategical importance, and military strength, of Strasbourg, Bitche, and Metz; the variety of the manufactures, and of the agricultural resources, of the country round Metz; and, more than all this wealth and strength, the people themselves of these districts, who were the manliest, the most industrious, and the most thriving part of the population of France. One can, at present, hardly estimate rightly the value of what has thus been taken from France, and given, if the expression may be allowed, to her natural enemy. Still it was France herself that laid this incalculable stake upon the table: her portion of the left bank of the Rhine against Prussia's; and insisted on the game being played. And the chances were against her. She had acquired Strasbourg by amazing treachery; and now the ignorance, arrogance, and vice by which she was to lose it, were equally amazing. And this war of 1870–71 was a natural sequel of the wrongs the first Napoleon did to Germany. That it was that had obliged the Germans to devote themselves to military organisation, and to understand the necessity of national union; and which was hardening their will, and nerving their arm. As to the French, one would be glad to find that they were delivering themselves from those causes in themselves, which led to their great catastrophe. But the existing generation cannot expect to see the day, when the rural population of France will have attained to more enlightenment than they have at present, and its city population to more rational ideas of liberty, justice, and truth, than they have exhibited hitherto; for the lives of the former are too hard, and the latter are too fanatical, to admit of much immediate improvement in either.

I stopped at Metz to see the battle-field of Gravelotte. I went over it with two Englishmen, who had come to Metz for the same purpose. We were provided with maps, and plans, and narratives of the great battle. It was a bright fine day. We started at 8.30 A.M., and did not get back to Metz till 5 P.M. It requires, at least, six hours to go over the field, including the hour you stop at Ste. Marie aux Chênes for baiting your horses, and for luncheon.

The French ground was well chosen for a defensive battle. It was along the ridge of the rising ground, facing to the west, from St. Privat and Roncour on their right, to the high ground opposite to, and behind St. Hubert, on their left. St. Hubert was a farmhouse in the depression. It had a walled garden. This ground was about five miles in length. Early in the day the Germans occupied only a part of the ground in front of the French position, beginning at Gravelotte, a little to the south-west of the French left. At this time there was no enemy in front of the French right. The ground here, rendered strong by a line of detached farm-houses, woods, and villages, was occupied by French outposts. From all these they were driven, in succession, by the extension of the German left. The strongest position here, and in it much hard fighting took place, was the village of Ste. Marie aux Chênes. The Germans first attacked the French left at St. Hubert. From this they drove them out. One can hardly understand how they managed to get possession of it, for the French occupied the high ground all round it. To march upon it was like marching into the bottom of a bowl to attack a strong place in the bottom, commanded by the enemy's cannon from every part of the rim. Having, however, established themselves here, they advanced up the hill against the French left. But, though they were repulsed, they were not driven out of St. Hubert. In the evening, the Germans, having established themselves along the front of the French right, and having even somewhat outflanked it, attacked them at St. Privat and Roncour. Here was most desperate fighting; and one, while standing on the ground, is surprised that any troops could have faced what the Germans had to go through. Their advance was made up a perfectly smooth, and open, incline, three-quarters of a mile across, the whole of it completely swept, and commanded by the French cannon, mitrailleuse, and Chassepots, which we must recollect killed some hundreds of yards further than the needle-gun. A Saxon corps, that had been coming up with forced marches, in the evening reached this point, and went straight up the hill. In fourteen minutes half its strength was *hors du combat.* There is a monument on the spot to those who fell here. The whole field is full of German monuments, for wherever their men fell, there they were buried ; and there a monument has since been raised to their memory. At last the French right was driven off this ground, and out of the strong village of St. Privat behind it. It was now dark. The French were in no position, or condition, to renew the fight the next day ; and so, during the night, they withdrew to Metz, leaving their material behind. They had fought a defensive battle, which suited neither the character of their troops, nor the circumstances of their position.

At Ste. Marie aux Chênes, where we stopped an hour for luncheon, we spent part of the time in walking about the village, and looking at the traces of the fight. It is a large village, every house of which has thick rubble or stone walls. All the buildings in it were occupied strongly by the French ; and all were, successively, carried. It was a from house-to-house and hand-to-hand fight. We found all the doors, window-shutters, and window-frames in the place, new, because the old ones had been battered in, hacked to pieces, and destroyed by the Germans, as they forced their way into each house separately. No prisoners were taken.

Among other spots we visited here was a little enclosed space, where the Germans had buried their dead. While we were looking at the grave of a young

Englishman of the name of Annesly—Von Annesly he is called on the stone—who had fallen in the assault on the village—he had attained to the rank of lieutenant in the German service—an elderly peasant woman approached; and, on finding that we were not Germans, freely entered into conversation with us. She soon told us that she was the mother of the Curé of the village. She had been one among the few inhabitants of the place, who, having taken refuge in cellars, had remained in it during the assault. She was very communicative, and invited us to accompany her to her house, where she showed us, with touching pride, their best tea service, and the church ornaments, which are used on fête days. The best room in the house had been appropriated to their safe keeping, and exhibition. The china service had been a present, what we should call a testimonial, and was placed, *en évidence*, on a table in the middle of the room. The church ornaments were arranged on a large sofa. They consisted of artificial flowers moulded in porcelain, with a great deal of gilding. The good woman then took us into the study; M. le Curé's study, as she was careful to tell us. She never referred to M. le Curé, and her thoughts were never far from him, without a smile of satisfied motherly emotion playing over her face. Those were M. le Curé's books. There were about half-a-dozen. That was the table at which M.

le Curé sometimes wrote. That garden, the outer door of the study opened upon it, was a beautiful garden, which M. le Curé worked in himself. M. le Curé was now absent from home, for the purpose of making a collection for the purchase of a figure of the Virgin, to commemorate her goodness in having miraculously saved the Church, when so much injury had been done to every other building in the place: but the church in the neighbouring village we saw had been burnt during the assault upon it. The good villagers had been very liberal in their contributions for the purchase of the figure. The sum, however, mentioned as their contributions, amounted only to a few francs. Still it might have been much for them to give, for they may not have been much in the habit of giving. M. le Curé's study, the scene of his peaceful and sacred studies, had been made a hospital. There, just where he always sits, a limb had been amputated. Here, and there, on the floor wounded men had died. The floor of M. le Curé's study had been stained with blood. One memento of that fearful day had been preserved. It was a small hole in the door through which a bullet had passed: but that was a bullet that had hurt nobody. I shall never think of the field of Gravelotte without a pleasing recollection of the mother of the Curé of Ste. Marie aux Chênes. She was a tall woman with what seemed a hard face, but at every mention of M. le Curé, or of the Holy

Virgin, it was lighted up, and softened. She wore a faded cotton dress, and a weather-stained, coalscuttle-shaped straw bonnet—her grandmother, perhaps, had once been proud of it—but the reflection of her simple, motherly, happy heart on her face, refined both face and dress. The heart's ease only was noticed.

The Germans have done, and are doing, everything that could be done, to restore to the people what they lost during the war. They have, in these parts, repaired every house and building that admitted of repair; and completely rebuilt all that had been too much injured for repair. They have thus given many new lamps for very old ones. They have not yet rebuilt the Church of St. Privat, because the people themselves have not yet decided, whether they wish the new one to be the fac-simile of the old one, or a larger structure, such as the increased population of the modern village requires: the familiar opposition between those who are afraid to acknowledge that the world has made any advances, and those who see nothing objectionable in advances, or in accommodating themselves to them. Of the other injuries, the people in these parts had sustained by the war, they were asked to make an estimate themselves. Half of their estimates was immediately paid to them; and they were told that the remaining half would be paid, after the 1st of October, on their having decided to become German citizens. The inhabitants of the villages round Metz had had their corn, and cattle, and horses swept off by the French Commissariat. These poor people the Germans fed during the siege with provisions brought from Germany. I could not hear in Metz, or in the neighbourhood, of a single instance of a German soldier having been seen drunk, or that any act of violence could be charged against them; nor could I hear even of oppression or harshness of any kind.

Metz, with its central arsenal, and its outer circle of apparently impregnable hill fortresses, gives you the idea of a place which nature had formed expressly for this gunpowder era, intending that its owners should fortify it, and use it as a rallying place for defeated armies—the armies, not of a small, but of a great nation; where they might in safety collect their shattered fragments; and, having re-organised and re-equipped themselves, might again take the field for fresh efforts. In the days of bows and spears it could not have had this value, which it may lose when our present instruments of war shall have been superseded by discoveries not yet dreamt of; but, although the French were not able to turn the place to such an account, still this seems to be one of the uses that may be made of it by its possessors: besides being an impregnable advanced post for the invasion of a neighbour.

. The Cathedral is far too short for its height. It contains some windows of very good old stained glass.

The only person I saw in it was an American. Shall I say that we had both come to see it, just as we might go to see some curious object in a museum? I, at all events, accused myself of something of this kind, for I had a consciousness of the discord between such a purpose, and the history and character of the structure. For however much it may now have the appearance of a thing unused, and unloved, and from which the soul has fled, yet was it built to satisfy a want, in the religious order, which all men longed to satisfy; and to give visible expression to a feeling, which then stirred every heart. Not anything else, not money, not power, could have built it; that is to say, could have summoned into existence the sentiments, of which the building is an embodiment.

But on this occasion its clustered columns, its groined roof, its lofty aisles, its jewelled light, transported my thoughts only to Mr. Spurgeon's Tabernacle; for I found myself endeavouring to understand and measure the difference between the two: but the endeavour brought me to see, under so much outward diversity, only an inward identity. They are both equally the result of the desire to form elevated and right conceptions of God—the focal name in which all elevated and right conceptions meet; and so to open the heart and mind, as that these elevated and right conceptions, which have been projected from them, may react upon them. This is Religion, the Spiritual life, in their simplest expression, in their inner form. In the ages of Faith, as they have been called, the most effectual way of attaining the desired end was through the eye; that is to say, the means, that could then be used with most effect, was art, in architecture, sculpture, painting, music. In the then state of the heart and of the imagination these best stirred and attuned them. Hence the Cathedral, and all that is implied in it. In these days, not of the knowledge, or of the conditions of life, or of the faith, of the old kinds, the most effectual means, especially among the lower strata of the middle class, is not art, which would have no power over them, but such direct appeals to their understandings and consciences, as will not be beyond their capacities. Hence Mr. Spurgeon and his Tabernacle. But the object is in both one and the same.

No sooner, however, had I come to this, which seemed for a moment to be a conclusion, than my thoughts entered the reverse process, and the identity I had been contemplating was transformed into diversity. The juxtaposition, in the mind's eye, of the Cathedral and of the Tabernacle suggested a difference, if not in the elements of religion itself, yet, at all events, in the modes through which different religious systems have attempted to act on the world. The Cathedral seemed to represent two modes : that which may for convenience be called, using the word in a good sense, the heathen mode; that is to say, culture, but in the form only of art; and the priestly, or Judaical, mode, which means organization. Its grand and beautiful structure grew out of the former, through the aid of the latter. The Tabernacle represents a totally different mode—the prophetical; and prophesying is the principle of life, of growth, and of development in religion. We see this throughout the history both of the Old and of the New Dispensation. Romanism has killed this vital principle; and is, therefore, as good as, or worse than, dead; for it has a bad odour. It is now all dead heathenism, and dead organization: a gilt and gaily painted monstrous iron machine, which can be set at work, but which has no heart. This explains everything. This is the key that unlocks its whole modern history. Its long ghastly list of persecutions, its Inquisition, its St. Bartholemew's, its Infallible Monocracy, are all alike logically deducible from the determination to live by other means than that of prophesying; in fact, utterly to suppress the one means of life, and to live, if such a thing were possible, by those means only which have not life in themselves. But Persecutions, Inquisitions, St. Bartholemew's, and Infallibility can be of no avail: for prophesying has always and everywhere been, and will always and everywhere be, the life of religion; and, therefore, destructive, sooner or later, of all cast-iron systems. With respect to the Tabernacle, it is not so much that it has rejected the

R

other two modes, as that it has no comprehension of their nature and use. It never, therefore, has either risen to the level of ordinary culture, or organized itself as a religious system. It makes no appeal to the former, and, Wesleyanism excepted, no use of the latter. This explains why, though not devoid of life, it is without form, and without attractive power for refined minds. Christianity, it is evident, in its early days depended entirely on prophesying. As it grew, having at that time the living power of assimilating what it needed, it borrowed organization from Judaism, and culture and art from heathenism: but prophesying must always be the distinctively Christian mode; so long as Christianity addresses itself to what is in man, that is, to his knowledge and moral consciousness.

Which, therefore, of these modes is the best is an inquiry, which would be somewhat sterile, and misleading; for each is good in its proper place, and degree, and for its proper purpose; and under some circumstances one, and under other circumstances another, will inevitably be resorted to. It would be more profitable to keep in mind that not one is ever exempt in its use from error and perversion. These, at every turn and step, will reappear, as the unavoidable results of the imperfections of those, in whose hands the administration of religion, as of all human affairs, must rest: for they are but men; and, Error and Perversion, you both have the same name, and that name is Man. History, and experience, teach us that, in the long run, the most efficient check to these errors and perversions, both in those who minister, and in those who are ministered to, is, as far as is possible in this world of necessarily mixed motives, and defective knowledge, to be dead unto self, and alive unto God, that is to the good work one finds set before one. Herein is the true apostolism: not for self, but for the end for which one was sent—for an object, beyond self, distinctly seen, and distinctly good. This in an individual is almost, and in a body of men perhaps quite, impossible. Still it is just what always has to be done by 'the Church,' which, in whatever sense we take the word, will be a body of men; and by Mr. Spurgeon, acting with those who believe in him; and, therefore, whenever attempted, will only be done very imperfectly. So it must be. But we see that, notwithstanding, the world has advanced, and is advancing. In 'the Church,' and among the Spurgeons and their respective people, and among others, who cannot be quite correctly ranged under either of these categories, there will always be some (generally a very small minority; but these are not questions that can be decided by counting hands) who have caught partial glimpses of what ought to be said and done, and who will set themselves the task, generally a very thankless one, of making their partial glimpses known. One thing, however, at all events is certain: it is safer to trust to the Spirit of the Prophet than to the culture and organization of the Priest, if they must be had separately: though, perhaps, their due combination, might be best of all.

These were the thoughts which passed through my mind, while I was in the Cathedral of Metz; for the American, who came in just after I had entered it, required but a very few minutes for 'doing' this grand old monument of mediæval piety; and soon left it to the twilight—the day was nearly run out—and to my twilight meditations.

The Hotel de l'Europe, the best in Metz, is not good. The head-waiter—he was an Austrian—was so imperious that I soon found it advisable, whenever I had occasion to ask him a question, to apologise for the trouble I was giving him. The angular peg had been put into the round hole. Nature had intended him for a German prince. They charge here for a two-horse carriage to Gravelotte, including the driver, two Napoleons. At this rate they must get back, one would think, every week the original cost of the rickety vehicle and half-starved horses. There is, however, but little competition in the matter of the imperious waiter, and none at all in that of the costly carriage he provides for you.

At Metz, and I heard that it was so, generally, throughout both the annexed provinces, a great many people were desirous of selling their houses and land. There was not, however, by any means an equal number of people who were desirous of purchasing. This fewness of purchasers indicates the prevalence of an opinion that the loss of these provinces is far too great for France ever to acquiesce in; and that, therefore, she will, on the first opportunity that may offer, endeavour to recover them by the sword: in which case they will become the theatre of war. It is true that the course of events in the New World, as well as in the Old, has taught the present generation, very impressively, the lesson that what is expected is seldom what happens; still, one may say, of course with a strong feeling of the uncertainty of human affairs, that there is nothing apparent, at present, on the surface of things, to give rise to the supposition that a second reference, on the part of the French, to the arbitrament of the sword, would lead to a different issue from that which the first had. Empire is maintained, and retained, by the means by which it was obtained; and there seems no probability of Germany ever allowing herself to be caught napping; or of her strength, energy, and determination being sapped by national corruption. That is not a consummation which the solid character of the people renders at all likely. Even their rude climate, which, to some extent, forbids a life of sensuous and vicious self-indulgence, will, we may think, help them in the future to maintain the character, which has always distinguished them hitherto; it seems to make earnestness, and mental hardihood, natural to them. One's thoughts on this subject would be very much modified, if there were in France any symptoms, which might lead one to hope that she was 'coming to herself.'

On leaving Metz, by an early train, I had to form one in a scene of crowding and confusion greater than I had ever elsewhere encountered on that side of the Channel, except a few days before at Strasbourg, where it was as bad. We are often told that the advantage of the foreign system of over-administration is that everything of this kind is rendered impossible; but here it was all in excess. Tickets for all classes were issued by the same clerk, and for two trains at the same time, for one was to start only a few minutes before the other. Some people were pushing; some were in a high state of excitement. There was no possibility of forming a *queue*. I was told that this, and many other things of the same kind, would be set right after the 1st of October, on which day the Germans would take all these matters into their own hands. Hitherto they had interfered with the local administration as little as possible. One consequence of this had been that the existing authorities, whose reign was so soon to expire, had not been very attentive to their duties; perhaps they had not been very desirous of keeping things straight; and the lower orders, availing themselves of the license that had been permitted, had become so insubordinate, that it had been found difficult, in some cases impossible, to carry on the operations of factories, in which many hands were employed. But after the 1st of October there was to be an end of all this: a German burgomaster was to be appointed, and German order was to be maintained. On that morning I wished that, as far as the station at Metz was concerned, the change had already been effected.

In the neighbourhood of Luxembourg, I saw several trains full of iron ore. From Luxembourg to Namur the country is, generally, very poor. It consists mainly of limestone hills, heaths, and woods in which there is little or no good timber. Between Namur and Brussels the country improves, agriculturally, very much.

At Brussels I had some difficulty in getting a bed; all the hotels being full of Belgian and English volunteers, and of people who had come to see the international shooting. There had just been a public reception of volunteers, and everybody was in the streets. I heard a burly tradesman, who was standing at the door of his shop, shout at the top of his voice, but the result did not correspond with the effort, as one of our volunteers was passing, in the uniform of a Scottish corps, 'Shotland for ever'—the land, doubtless, of good shots. Etymologists, consider this, and be cautious.

The much-lauded Hotel de Ville I venture to

think unsatisfactory. For so much ornamentation it is deficient in size. Its chief external feature is the multitude of figures upon it. The effect of this is bad. One sees no reason why they should be there. They are too small. They are indistinguishable from each other. There is no action : merely rows of figures. This was unavoidable in the position assigned them, but its being unavoidable was no reason for assigning them that position, nor does it at all contribute towards rendering them pleasing objects.

Many of the volunteers made a night of it in honour of their English visitors. Having been woke, by their shouting and hurraing in the streets, at one o'clock in the morning, I was disposed to think such demonstrations unbecoming in bearded warriors.

I went with a party of Englishmen, and some Americans, to Waterloo. We were driven over the old, straight, stone-paved, poplar-bordered road, by an English whip, in an English four-horse stage-coach. The road is just what it was, when Wellington passed over it, from 'the revelry at night' for the great fight. That part, however, of the Forest of Soignies, which should be on the right of the road, has been destroyed, to make way for the plough. What remains of the forest, on the left, consists of tall, straight, unbranching beech, with the surface of the ground, between the trunks, clear and smooth. While we were at Hougomont a violent thunderstorm, accompanied with heavy rain, drifted over the field. As the soil is a tenacious clay, which becomes very slippery when wet, this storm was most opportune, for it showed us what kind of footing the contending hosts had on the great day. Hougomont is still very much in the condition in which it was left on the evening of that day. What was burnt has not been rebuilt; and what remained, has not been added to, or altered. The loop-holes that were made in the garden wall are still there. So also are the hedge, and ditch, on the outside of the orchard. The only difference is that the whole of the wood of Hougomont has gone the way of a part of the Forest of Soignies. We have all of us tried to understand Waterloo; but a visit to the field itself will show that it is no more possible to understand, fully and rightly, this than any other battle, without ocular knowledge of the ground on which it was fought. A comparison of the field of Waterloo with that of Gravelotte will assist a civilian in estimating the extent of the change in tactics, which modern improvements in the weapons of war have necessitated. He will see that the battle of June 18, 1815, belongs to an order of things that is obsolete now. With the cannon, and rifles, of the present day, it could not have been fought as it was; and would not, probably, have been fought where it was.

CHAPTER XVIII.

HOW THE OBSERVATION AND KNOWLEDGE OF NATURE, AND THE CONDITIONS OF SOCIETY AFFECT RELIGION AND THEOLOGY. AN INSTRUCTIVE PARALLELISM. CONCLUSION.

Consider the lilies of the field.—*Gospel of St. Matthew.*
The powers that be are ordained of God.—*Epistle to the Romans.*

IT was 8 o'clock in the evening when I left Brussels. At 6 o'clock the next morning I stepped upon the platform of the Charing Cross Station. So ended, after very nearly five weeks, my little excursion. In the foregoing pages I have set down, not only what I saw, which could not have had much novelty, but the thoughts, also, as well about man as about nature, which what I saw suggested to me; and these, too, may not have much value. To some, however, everything in nature is instructive and interesting, and so is everything in man; or they seem to be so. But, in order to secure this instruction and interest, I believe that they must be viewed connectedly. The one is properly intelligible only by the light that shines from the other. To regard either separately is to misunderstand both. Nature is the field in which He, Whose form no man hath seen at any time, reveals to us His Creative Power, for the purpose that the intelligent contemplation of the objects, He presents to our view, should engender in us certain sentiments and ideas, which have from the beginning, in the degree and form possible at each epoch, underlaid religion. Our fellow men are the field in which He reveals to us the capacities and conditions; the strength, the weaknesses, the workings, and the aspirations of moral and of intellectual being, as conditioned in ourselves: another, and perhaps a higher, revelation of Himself; and the consciousness of which being in the individual constitutes, as far as we know, in this visible world of ours, the distinctive privilege of man; and the exercise of which, under the sense of responsibility, crowns the edifice of religion. The study of both has been equally submitted to us, is equally our duty, and is necessary for the completion of our happiness. They are the correlated parts of a single revelation, and of a single study. The man who shuts his eyes to the one, or to the other, cannot understand, at all events as fully as he might, either that portion of the revelation at which he looks exclusively, or himself, or Him, Who makes the revelation, in the sense in which He has willed that each should be understood.

The products of our modern advanced methods of agriculture bear the same kind of relation to the products of the burnt stick (they could both support life, but very differently), that the religious sentiments and ideas produced by our knowledge of nature bear to those which the ignorant observation of a few prominent phenomena, as thunder and lightning, the power of the wind and of the sun, the action of fire, life and death, produced in the minds of the men of that remote day. The mind of the inhabitants of this country, precisely like the land of this country, was just the same at that day as at this. The powers and capacities of each are invariable. What varies, and always in the direction of advance, is that which is applied to the mind: as is the case also with respect to the land. The knowledge of what produces the thunder and lightning, of the laws that govern the motions of the heavenly bodies, of what originates and calms the wind, of the forces of nature, of the structure of animals and plants, are so many instruments, by which the constant quantity, the human mind, is cultivated for greater productiveness. No one dreams that we have approached the end of such knowledge, any more than that our agriculture has reached its last advance. The state of knowledge, whatever it may be at any time (from that of our rudest forefathers to our own), produces corresponding ideas and sentiments. Its reception into the mind unfailingly generates those ideas and sentiments, just as the application of any method of agriculture, with the appliances that belong to it, gives the amount and kind of produce from the land proper to that method and to those appliances. As an instance taken from a highly civilized people, the close observation of the instincts of animals, and of the properties of plants, offered to the leisure, accompanied by some other favouring circumstances, of the ancient Egyptians, but unaccompanied by any knowledge of the laws, the forces, and the order of nature ; that is to say, their existing knowledge, together with the existing limitations to that knowledge, led unavoidably to the ideas and sentiments we find in them ; that is to say, to what was their religion, which combined the worship of plants and animals, with belief in a future life.

The other self-acting factor to that organization of thought and sentiment, which is religion, is the observation of what will perfect human society, and the life of the individual, under the conditions of their existence at the time. Certain things ought to be removed : it is religion to remove them. Certain things ought to be maintained : it is religion to maintain them. Certain things ought to be established : it is religion to establish them. Certain knowledge ought to be propagated : it is religion to propagate it.

Now both these contributions to religion, the

knowledge of nature, which is inexhaustible, and the conditions of human society, which are endlessly multiform, are progressively variable quantities; religion, therefore, the resultant of the combined action of the two, must itself vary with them; that is to say, must advance with them.

It is a corollary to this, that from the day a religion forms itself into a completed system, it becomes a matured fruit; the perfected result of a train of anterior and contemporary conditions, that have long been working towards its production. Thenceforth it is useful for a time just as a fruit may be. It has, also, in itself, as a fruit has, the seed of a future growth. But with that exception, though still serviceable, it is dead, though organized, matter. A certain concurrence of conditions, which can never be repeated, because knowledge and society are ever advancing, produced the fruit, which, like that of the aloe, can only be produced once out of its own concurrence of conditions. Man's spiritual nature feeds on that fruit, and is nourished by it, for a greater or less number of generations. At last, for it must come, a new concurrence of conditions arises, and a new fruit is produced. The vital germ that was in the old fruit, passed into the *milieu* of the new ideas and sentiments, and a new growth commenced. Organization then ensued, and in due time bore, as its fruit, its own matured and perfected system. At the establishment of Christianity, in the order of knowledge, the perception of the absurdity of thousands of local divinities, and, in the social and political order, the establishment of an Universal Empire, which gave rise to a sense of the brotherhood of mankind, combined in demanding that the whole organization of religious thought should be recast. Everyone can see the part these two facts had in the construction, and in bringing about the reception, of Christian ideas and Christian morality. In these days we see that social and political conditions are changing, though we cannot so exactly define and describe in what that change consists as we can that just referred to; but we know that at the time of that change there was, though it was distinctly felt, the same absence of power to define and describe it distinctly. About the recent advance, however, in knowledge there is no want of distinctness: that is as palpable as it is, beyond measure, greater than the advances of all former times. It amounts almost to a revelation of the constitution and order of nature. The ideas and sentiments this new knowledge has given rise to are somewhat different from, for instance they are grander and give more satisfaction to thought than, the ideas and sentiments that accompanied the knowledge, or rather the ignorance, on the same subjects, of two, or of one, thousand years back. This must have some effect on the religion of Christendom, and the effect cannot but be elevating and improving. This knowledge cannot possibly be bad, because it is only the attainment of the ideas, which, on the theory both of religion and of commonsense, were in the mind of the Creator before they were embodied in nature ; which were embodied in nature, and were submitted to us, in order that they might be attained to by us, for the sake of the effect the knowledge would have upon our minds, that is to say, ultimately on our religion.

This knowledge, it is notorious, is not estimated in this way by many good men amongst us, they, on the contrary, being disposed to regard it rather with repugnance, horror, and consternation. The reason is not far to seek. They have, probably, in all such cases, received only a theological and literary training. Now every theology, as is seen in the meaning of the word, and as belongs to the nature of the construction, contains an implicit assertion, both that no new knowledge, which can have any good influence on men's thoughts, sentiments, and lives, can be attained, subsequently to the date of its own formation ; and that the workings of human society will never lead to advances beyond those, which had at that time been reached. And literary training, in this country, has hitherto meant a kind of *dilettante* acquaintance with the literature of the ancient Greeks and Romans, regarded, not as a chapter in the moral and intellectual history of the race, but rather as supplying models for expression. No wonder, then, need be felt at finding those, who are conversant only with what is dead, scared at the phenomena of life. The wonder would be if it were otherwise. But the same conditions, we all know, act differently on differently constituted minds: and this explains the opposite effect which modern criticism has upon the minds of some of those who have had only literary training. This criticism they find opposed to some of the positions of the old theology; and the effect of this discovery upon them is that it makes them hostile to religion itself. As well might Newton have felt horror at the idea of gravitation because Ptolemy had believed in cycles and epicycles. It is the preponderance of literary training in them, also, that issues in this opposite result.

Religion is the organization of all that men know both of outward nature and of man, for the purpose of guiding life, of perfecting the individual and society, and of feeding the mind and the heart with the contemplation of the beauty and order of the universe, inclusive of man and of God, that is to say, of the conception we can form, at the time, of the All-originating, All-ordering, and All-governing Power. This is, ever has been, and ever will be Religion, unless we should pass into a New Dispensation, at present inconceivable, because it would require the recasting, at all events, of man, if not of the external conditions of his existence, that is, of the world also. But as long as things continue as they have been, knowledge will always advance religion; and religion will always conform itself to knowledge. The essential difference between one religion and another, from Fetishism up to Christianity, is one of knowledge.

Before the construction of systematic theologies, knowledge and religion were convertible terms. It was so under the Old Dispensation; and so again in the early days of Christianity. After their construction the former term was modified. It had been generic, it thenceforth became specific. The differentiating limitation imposed upon it was that of this particular theology, exclusive of all other theologies; and, as it was a theology, this involved the exclusion of the ideas of correction and enlargement.

Error and insufficiency must, from the nature of the materials dealt with, after a time be found in every theology. In this sense every Church has erred, and could not but have erred. The mischief, however, is not in this error and insufficiency, for they are remediable. The progress of knowledge which points out the error, often indeed creating it by the introduction of additional data, supplies the means for correcting it; and the advance in the conditions of society, which creates the insufficiency, suggests the means for correcting it, too. Nor, again, is the mischief in the ignorance of the majority, for that can to the extent required be removed. It is in the determination of some, from whom better things might have been expected, not to examine all things with the intention of holding fast that which is true; but to close their eyes and ears, as theologians, against all that the educated world now knows, and all that the uneducated masses are repelled by in what is now presented to them as the Word of God. This determination puts them in the position of being obliged to support, and encourage, only those who address themselves to the ignorance of the age, but not for the purpose of removing it; and to oppose, and discourage, those who address themselves to the knowledge of the age, for the purpose of making it religious. We need not repeat what we have been told will happen, when the blind lead the blind.

The recollection of what has given to our political constitution its orderly and peaceful development might be of use here. It goes on accommodating itself smoothly, and without convulsions, to the altering conditions of society, because political parties amongst us are not coincident with classes. Members of the popular party are to be found in the highest classes as well as in the lowest, and of the stationary party in the lowest as well as in the highest. This is what has here exorcized the demon of revolution. If party lines had been drawn horizontally instead of vertically, class would have been arrayed against class; and, probably, ignorance and violence, supported by numbers, would have made a clean sweep of our institutions, and, to no small extent, of our civilization. What has been advantageous in the political order would be equally so in the religious. What has saved us from a political, might, if adopted, save us from a possible religious, crash. It is a miserably short-sighted policy to endeavour to drive from the camp of religion, or of the National Church, those who have accepted the knowledge of our times, and who have sympathies with the existing tendencies or possibilities of society: so that on one side shall be arrayed only those, who rest on what is old, and on the other only those, who have no disposition to reject what is new. Whereas the true bridge from the present to the future can be constructed by neither of these parties alone; but must be the work of those, whose wish and effort are to combine, and to harmonise, the new with the old. This appreciation of what is needed, is, at all events, in accordance with the meaning of the saying, to the authority of which we must all defer, that 'every scribe, who is instructed unto the Kingdom of Heaven, will bring forth out of his treasures things new as well as old.' The course taken by those, who lose sight of the guidance offered them in this saying, can only bring them into a false position.

It is very instructive to observe how circumstances analogous to those, which existed among the chosen people, at the date of the promulgation of Christianity, are, at this moment, amongst ourselves producing analogous effects. We have lately heard those, who are attempting to make the knowledge, men have now been permitted to attain to, an element of religion, which is what knowledge must always become in the end, described as 'maudlin sentimentalists.' Precisely the same expression, motived by precisely the same feelings, and ideas, might have been applied with the same propriety, or impropriety, and with the same certainty of disastrous recoil on those who used it, to the teaching of the Divine Master Himself. He appealed from the hard, narrow, rigid forms, in which the old Law had been fossilized, to the sense men had come to have of what was moral, and needed, and to the knowledge they had come to have of what was true, under the then advanced conditions of society and of knowledge. The maintainers of the fossilized Law were for binding heart and mind fast in the fetters of dogmatic human traditions. He was for setting mind and heart free by the reception of what was broad and true; at once human and divine. That alone was desirable, beneficent, and from God. It blessed, strengthened, emancipated, and gave peace. No authority, however venerable, could be pleaded against it. No thrones, principalities, or powers, however exalted, would be able to withstand it. There was no fear or possibility of its being refuted: for it was nothing but the perception, and the practical recognition, of existing knowledge, and of existing conditions. Men, they might be many, might reject it, but to their own detriment only. The facts would remain. The rest, all whose eyes were open, or could be opened, to perceive what was before their eyes, would receive it as from God. The more it was set in the broad light of day the better. It must be proclaimed in the highways, and the market-places, and in the Temple itself. If those who had received it were to hold their peace, the stones would immediately cry out. It was God's Truth. It was God's Word: not because it was written, for as yet it was not written, but because, as the Word of God ever had, and ever would, come, it came from the pure heart, and the enlightened understanding, and approved itself to those, who had eyes to see, and ears to hear, and hearts to understand. Let every one examine it. If in that day had been known what is now known of man's history, and of nature, and of what is seen of the possibility of raising men, throughout society, to a higher moral and intellectual level than was heretofore attainable, we may be sure that there would have been no attempt to discredit such knowledge, and such aspirations; and that they would have been urged as extending our knowledge of God, and of His will; that they would have been appealed to, and that men would have been called upon to raise themselves to the level of what had become conceivable, and, conceivably, attainable. At all events, the one great point, the one paramount duty, was to proclaim what was then seen to be true. To keep back nothing. To care nothing for the consequences, in the way of what it might overthrow; to be ready to spend and be spent for the consequences, in the way of the good it must produce. The requisite boldness would come to its promulgators from feeling, that it was God's work, and that He was on their side. The issue could not be doubtful. The Gates of Hell could not prevail against the Truth. It was, notwithstanding its 'maudlin sentimentality,' mighty to the pulling down of strongholds; and went forth conquering, and to conquer. So will it do again. So will it do ever. The parallelism is complete at every point. It is only strange that it has not been seen, and dwelt upon, till all have become familiar with it. The facts, the situation, the ideas, the hopes and fears, are the same. So, too, is the language needed to describe them, each and all.

The thoughts, which this chapter outlines, were often, as might be supposed, in my mind during the little excursion described in the foregoing pages. They are, as far as I can see, the logical and inevitable conclusions of the acquaintance some have, such as it may be, with history and with physical science; and I suppose that travelling further along the same road would only enable them to see the object to which it leads with more distinctness. In Switzerland there is much both in the singularly varied mental condition of the people themselves, and in the impressive aspects of nature, to confirm them. The narrative, though its form, in keeping with the particular purpose in which it originated, is at times somewhat minute, may yet, as things were, for the most part, seen and regarded through the medium of ideas I have just referred to, contribute a little to their illustration. It was my wish, at all events, that my mind and heart should be always open, unreservedly, to the teaching of all that I saw, both of man and of nature; but still, I trust, with that caution, and sense of responsibility, that befit the formation of opinions, by which—for one is conscious that they are the inner man, the true self—one must stand, or fall, and in which one must live, and die.

INDEX.

AAR

AAR, 150-2
Aigle, 183
Absenteeism, 43
Agriculture, capital improves, 60. In the United States, 69. Burnt stick and hoe eras, 81. Progress in size of farms, 83-5. In Alsace, 230
American lads mountaineering, 13
Americans in Switzerland, 200
Animal worship, rationale of, in the ancient Egyptians, 253
Antithesis, an Alpine, 13
Anza, 126
Apostolism, true, 243
Armies of the Romans, 141
Art, place of, in religion, 241
Auroch, 212
Austrian marriages, 100. Waiter, 244
Avalanches, 22, 158

BLUE boy, 13, 16, 141, 142, 154, 163, 164, 171, 184-193
Bonus amicus pro vehiculo, 133
Breakfast at a monster hotel, 195
Bridge, from the present to the future, 260
Brieg, 140
Brienz, 155
Brussels, 247. Hôtel de Ville, unsatisfactory, 248

CHR

Bubble schemes why alluring, 67
Buffers, our labourers have three, 105, 106
Butterflies, 53, 151

CAMPING out, 177
Capital, power of, in modern societies, 50. Revolution effected by, 53. Inversion of land and, 54. Peel and Gladstone, due to, 55. A ladder, 56. Era of, on Visp-side, 50-66. Will improve agriculture, 61. Flow of, to the land will counterbalance cities, 62. Moral and intellectual effects, 63. Increases size of agricultural concerns, 85. Size of estates in era of, 94. Is king, 103. Essence of all property, 106, 107. Uses of, discriminated, 108, 109
Carpet, magical bit of, 3
Caterpillar, 53, 127
Cathedral of Metz, 238-242
Ceppo Morelli, 127
Certificates of land-shares, 87, 89, 93, 94
C'est un pauvre pays, 217
Change, modern craving for, 4, 5
Christianity, in what sense a recast of religious thought, 255. A

CHU

modern parallel to the ground taken by first promulgators of, 261-3
Church, value of establishment, 65. Effect of disestablishment, 97
Cities, land counterpoise to, 62; and land, 93
Classics, place of, in English education, 222, 223. Unfairly weighted, 226
Colmar and Mulhouse, cotton industry of, 230
Continuity of human history, 213
Co-operation inapplicable to land, 104-6
Corporate estates, 74, 76, 96
Cost of Swiss travel, 176
Coups manqués of humanity, 202
Cranoges, Irish and Scotch, 210
Curé of Sainte Marie aux Chênes, 235

DANUBE, Roman road on the banks of the, 126
Dinner, last, in London, 3. At Macugnaga, 125. At a monster hotel, 196
Disorder, temporary, permitted at Strasbourg and Metz, 246
Distel, 122
Dogs, why bay the moon, 181
Domo D'Ossola, 128
Drama of the Mountains, 184-193
Drunkenness, how may be discouraged, 85. Want of drink-water a cause of, 209
Dust, 174

ECLIPSE, feelings caused by, 182
Edelweiss, 161
Education, property is an, 33. What would promote, 84. Spread of, unfavourable to

GAS

existing land-system, 97. Range and method of teaching, 192, 193. Swiss aims, 218-221. How applicable, and how not, to us, 221-223. Sciences of humanity needed, 221, 222. Imagination should be cultivated, 223. Place of poetry in, 224
Eggishhorn, 143
Elsass, agricultural wealth of, 230
Empire, how retained, 245
Enthusiastic ladies, 200
Establishments, religious, useful under landlordism, 65. Effect of disestablishment, 97
Etymology of field, 82. Of Scotland, 247
Expected, what is, seldom happens, 245
Eyes in back of the head, 97

FALLOWS abandoned, 83
Falls of Frosinone, 135. Another, 136. Aar and Handeck, 152. Staubbach, 152. Reichenbach, 154
Fee, 116
Field, etymology of, 82
Feudalism, none in our landlordism, 77
Findelen, 17
Fireworks at Interlaken, 164
Flies, 147
Flowers, 14, 18
France, a cause of its wealth, 98. Insisted on war, 231
French petty proprietors, 105, 106, 110
Frosinone, 135
Fruit, religion is a, 254
Fungus, a Brobdingnagian, 144

GAME, 82
Gasteren, 167

INDEX

GAU

Gauter, 139
Gemmi, 167–71
Geneva, Lake of, excavated by glacier, 8
Genius loci, 133
Geology of Rhone Valley, 7. Of Alpine valleys, 134. Of Delta of the Kander, 166
German professor, 114. Travellers, 156, 201. At Gravelotte, 232–6. At Metz, 237. Conquests will be retained, 245
Glacier action, 7. Bies, 9. Gorner, 9. Fee, 116. Allalein, 119. Kaltenwasser, 138. Rhone, 146. Old Aar, 150. Grindelwald, 162
Gladstone, the Right Hon. W. E., 55
Gneiss, channel how cut in, 151
God, the focal name, 239
Gondo, 135
Gorner Grat, 12
Government, modern Swiss, 146
Gravelotte, battle of, 232–6
Grimsel, 149
Grindelwald, 160
Guide, 18, 115, 123, 127
Guttanen, 153

HANDECK, 151, 152
Health, better to keep than to recover, 183
Helle Platte, 150
History, continuity of, 213
Homer, a simile of his, 178, 183
Honesty, 36, 39
Hornli, 17
Hospice, Simplon, 135. Grimsel, 148, 149
Hotels, St. Niklaus, 8. Riffel, 16. Saas, 115. Mattmark See, 120. Macugnaga, 125. Ponte Grande, 127. Domo D'Ossola, 128. Simplon, 135.

KNI

Du Glacier du Rhone, 147. Interlaken, 156. Grindelwald, 161. Schwarenbach, 168. Swiss monster hotels, 194–204. Zurick, 215. Metz, 244
Human interest of improved agriculture, 86
Humanity, sciences of, place in education, 221
Humility, true, 216

ICE sent from Grindelwald to Paris, 162. Ice-field of Bernese Oberland, 174
Ignorance of the day, some address themselves to, but not for the purpose of removing it, 259
Imagination, place in education, 223. How to be cultivated, 224
Imhof, 153
Industry, Swiss, 34–8, 46, 129
Intellectual life among peasant proprietors, 32. Under landlordism, 48. Under capital, 63, 107
Interlaken, 155, 156
Investments for all, 87, 88
Invidious position, 101, 102
Italians compared to Swiss, 129

JACK of many trades, 118
Joint-stock cultivation of the land, 78–89
Jungfrau, 156–8

KANDER, Delta of the, 166
Kandersteg, 167
King, capital is, 103
Kitchen-maids, acquisition and use of capital within reach of, 109
Knights' fees, number of, 77

KNO

Knowledge, what it is, 227. Grammatical and theological studies obscure, 229. Its effects on religion, 257

LAKE-VILLAGES, 210–215. Land, reclamation and cultivation of, 21. In Greece and Rome, 51. In feudal times, 52. Inversion of land and capital, 54. Settlement of, prevents distribution, 70. Joint-stock principle applicable to, 78. Land mobilised, 88. Increased value under joint-stock cultivation, 88, 89. Land and cities, 93. Size of landed estates in era of capital, 94. Might be sold subject to rent-charge, 95. Tendency of things with respect to; corporate estates, 96. Disestablishment, 97. Increasing size of estates, 97. Education, 97. Perception of cause of wealth of France, 98. Increase in our population and wealth, 98. Popular character of modern legislation, 99. Rise in cost of labour, 99. How two kinds of wills affect land, 110. Culture and price of, in Switzerland, 206

Landlordism, 41, 50. Political effects in Ireland and Scotland, 111

Landowners, advantage to, of joint-stock cultivation of the land, 89. Diminishing numbers, 97

Lausanne, 3
Lauterbrunnen, 157
Leukabad, 172–4
Life, who scared by phenomena of, 257
Literary and theological training, effects of, 256
Lords of creation, 124

NON

Lothringen, 231
Lowe, Right Hon. R., 65
Luxembourg, 247

MACUGNAGA, 125. Magician, capital a, 107
Man, conditions antecedent to, 116
Matterhorn, 12, 17, 18
Mattmark See, 119, 120
Meiringen, 153
Men and women highest form of wealth, 32
Methods of teaching, 192, 193
Metz, 230
Money lords, 55
Monte Leone, 138
Moon on the Jungfrau, 165. Witchery of the, 179. Why dogs bay, 181
Moral value of peasant-proprietorship, 34–40. Under landlordism, 46
Morality, man lives not only by or for, 40
Moro, Monte, 123
Mortmain, history of abolition of, 74. Its failure, 75
Mother of Curé of Ste. Marie aux Chênes, 235
Mountaineering, 10, 19, 20
Mountains seen face to face, 121
Munster, 144
Museum of Lake Villages, 210, 215
Myriad-minded, 223

NATURE, 192, 225. Nautical felicity, 6
New world's contributions to old, 7
Niesen, 175
Nonconformity, strength and weakness of, 241, 242

OBERWALD, 146
Opinion, how stream of tendency affects, 99
Organisation, religious, 241
Ownership of land, proposed form of, 89

PAGANISM, modern, 26
Parallelism of the present religious situation and that at the promulgation of Christianity, 261-3
Paris, 1
Parquetry flooring, 182
Pauper, euthanasia of agricultural, 86
Peak-climbers and pass-men, 10, 18, 175, 199
Peasant-proprietorship, 29-40. Impossible here, 94. French, 105, 106, 110
Pedestrianism, pedantry of, 144
Peel, Sir R., 55
Personal worth, 103
Physical science teaches what truth is, 228
Picturesque will not stop advances, 86
Pié de Muléra, 128
Pinus Cembra, 11, 159. Pumilio, 150
Platform road, 126
Poetry of Vale of Grindelwald, 161. Classical and modern, 224
Pompeii, 52
Ponte Grande, 127
Poor law, rationale of, 106
Population under peasant-proprietorship, 31. Under landlordism, 45
Porter and practical man, 156
Possibilities, 27
Post-office, Swiss, 118
Potatovors, Irish, 105, 106
Practical man and porter, 156

Prasias, Lake, 210
Prayers played for, 24
Primogeniture, 90
Property, educational effects of, 33
Prophesying, place of, in religion, 241, 242
Prospects of great proprietors, 100

RAILWAYS, delays on Swiss, 138
Recolte des voyageurs, 217
Reichenbach, falls of, 154
Religion, 25. Its primitive and modern forms, 145. Relation to art, organisation, and prophesying, 141, 142. Error and perversion in, 242, 243. Relation of the knowledge of nature and of man to, 251. How affected by the conditions of society, 253. Progressive, 254. A parellelism, 261-3
Religious establishments, when useful, 64
Rent-charge, land might be sold subject to, 95
Responsibility in the formation of opinions, 264
Revolution, a great but bloodless, 53
Rhone, Delta of Upper, 7. Source of, 146
Riffel, 11, 16
Rocky mountains, young pines in, 160. Camping-out in, 177
Romanism, decay of, 25, 26. How uses art, organisation, and prophesying, 241

SAAS, 113 121
Sac, lost, 131
St. Niklaus, 8, 21
Ste. Marie aux Chênes, fight in, 234. Mother of curé of, 235

INDEX

SAL

Saltine, 139
Saracens, 124
Savings' bank for all, 87, 109
Scene from Gorner Grat, 12. Valley of Saas, 113. Mattmark, 120. Macugnaga, 125. Gemmi, 169
Schwartz See, 16, 17
Scotland, a Belgian's etymology of, 247
Selborne, White of, 4. Lord, 4, 65
Self, when to be considered, 132. When not, 243
Sermon on the Riffel, 15. Effect of fluency and imagination on, 165
Settlement of land prevents distribution, 70. Action of settled estates, 72. How preventible, 73
Shawls, fine, better than rugs, 117
Simplon, 131-9
Size of estates in era of capital, 94
Slavery, 82
Society, conditions of, affect religion, 253
Sprite, the reprobate, 203
Spurgeon, Mr., 239, 243
Stalden, 113
Steam culture, 83
Stenches in hotels, 8, 147, 148
Stone age, 81, 211
Strasbourg, 230
Sugar factories, 84
Sun, colourless risings, 175. Of England has set, 202. A good sunset, 216, 217
Swiss life in a valley, 23, 29 40. Compared with Italians, 129. Monster hotels, 194-204. Swiss sights suggestive, 264

TEACHING, range and method of, 192. 193
Technical University of Zurich, 218

WAT

Tendency of events as respects land, 96
Tents, travelling with, in Switzerland, 177
Testimony, fallibility of, 118
Theology, 256
Thun, 163
Too soon but late at last, 168
Travel, order of, 5
Travellers in monster hotels, 198. Swiss, classified, 199 203
Trust-funds, investment proposed for, 89
Twice as clever, 171

UNITED STATES, answer to a question asked in the, 68
Agriculture of, 69
Urus, 212

VAL ANZASCA, 126, 129, 130
Valleys, geology of Alpine, 134. View of Grindelwald, 160
Venice, 210
Verrieres, 2
Villages of Upper Rhone Valley, 144. Old Lake, 210-215
Vines and vineyards, 205
Virgin, the Holy, at Ste. Marie aux Chênes, 236
Virtue, highest form of, 38
Visp, 8. Life and religion in Valley of the, 21-27. Thoughts about land suggested by the Valley of the, 28-112
Voiturier, boorish, 143. Dilatory, 165. Payment should depend on time, 166

WATER-SUPPLY in Switzerland, 206-9. In England, 207, 208. Would lessen drunkenness, 209
Waterloo, 248, 249

WEA

Weather, 175
Well-being, constituents of, 40
Wengern Alp, 157, 158
Wheat cultivated by Old Lake villagers, 212
White of Selborne, 4
Widows and younger children provided for by landowners, 93
Wife, 5, 142, 162, 168, 171
Wildstrubel, 169
Will strengthened, 139

ZUR

Wills, two errors with respect to, 110
Wine, 197
Wood carving, 155

ZERMATT, 9, 10, 115
Zmutt glacier, 17
Zurich Museum of lake village antiquities, 210–215. Modern city, 214. Technical University, 218

BY THE SAME AUTHOR.

The Duty and Discipline of Extemporary Preaching.

SECOND EDITION.

C. SCRIBNER & CO., NEW YORK.

A Winter in the United States:

Being Table-Talk collected during a Tour through the late Southern Confederation, the Far West, the Rocky Mountains, &c.

JOHN MURRAY, LONDON.

Egypt of the Pharaohs and of the Kedivé.

SECOND EDITION.   [In the Press.

SMITH, ELDER, & CO., LONDON.

www.ingramcontent.com/pod-product-compliance
Lightning Source LLC
Chambersburg PA
CBHW032102220426
43664CB00008B/1104